Acknowledgements

This collection of essays is the culmination of a semester's worth of diligent work by 18 students at Ozarks Technical Community College. Their time, effort, and rigorous exploration of the ideas contained in these essays were made much more meaningful by the support and contributions from the following people at OTC: Dr. Lance Renner, Dean of General Education; Dr. Matt Hudson, Dean of Technical Education; Mr. John Fishback, Department Chair of Biological Clinical Science; Mr. Jeff Johnson, Electronic Media Production Instructor.

The following student-authors also worked overtime as editors of their peers' writing: Cally Chisholm, Hannah Quick, Andrea Savage, Lane Williamson, and Hannah Winder. Students Kendra Caruso, Abby Cool, and Lane Williamson were instrumental in assembling the work for publication. Fellow English instructors Michael Borich and Jane Cowden were generous with their time and expertise in helping the students navigate the publication process. The combined efforts of these individuals helped turn the solitary work of the writers into the public offering of their talents and thoughtfulness which you can now enjoy. I'm grateful for that support and for the opportunity to work with such fine people.

Richard Turner

OTC English Department Chair

IDENTITY

REFLECTIONS ON THE SELF

OTC HONORS PROGRAM

Forward

One of the most prevalent clichés of our time is that technology is shrinking our world. With an act as simple as spitting into a plastic tube from a home DNA kit, we can initiate a process that allows us to delve into the most minuscule parts of ourselves, showing us in elegant clarity how stunningly alike and connected we all are, and always have been. And yet it's also no secret that technology can separate us. Isolate us. As our efforts to gather information, pursue truths, develop relationships, and process sense input about the outside world become increasingly virtual, do we run the risk of finding that our "selves" are also becoming somehow less authentic—more virtual—as well? In a 1922 poem, E. E. Cummings described the New England socialites as people who "live in furnished souls," content within their "comfortable minds." Thanks to the technology quite literally at our fingertips, it's vastly easier to gather information today than it was in 1922—or even a generation ago—but that same increase in the volume of *what* we can find makes it harder to know what to think *about* all that information we can so easily find. And the same effect may be happening with that slow and gradual process required to find and know ourselves.

Looking out at the world from a "furnished soul" or "comfortable mind" is certainly more . . . well, comfortable than willfully embracing the cognitive dissonance that comes from purposeful introspection— from looking within. But perhaps clarifying what we think we know about ourselves is a necessary first step in coming to know what we think about each other and the rest of our shrinking world. The writers who offer you their thoughts in the following pages have chosen to embrace that journey, and would be honored with your company.

Richard Turner

Table of Contents

Table of Contents

Discovering Self

Sarah Powell

The identity of self is sometimes difficult to define. There are many different components that influence each individual's identity: age, race, occupation, beliefs, and experiences. However, the most important aspect of identity is the perception of self and how that perception influences the way individuals react to the world around them.

Personally, I had never seriously considered the concepts of identity until I took an Honors English class at Ozarks Technical Community College. Nor did I have any inkling of what could transpire in that class during the semester. Far from just manufacturing essays for writing prompts, the class actively researched, studied, discussed, argued, and unearthed what the term "identity" of self truly means. With each writing project, we discovered what we personally believed identity is. In a twist of irony, because no one shared the same identity, each student focused on different components of identity.

However, we did not passively study this fascinating subject; we actively experienced it. To better understand the value of the concepts, we researched our family records to learn where our ancestors were from, our teacher invited one of the school's science professors to class to explain how genetics and DNA affect identity, we discussed the ideas that Jung and Freud had on identity, the class examined artwork and poetry to discover artists' ideas on identity, and we even had our DNA tested to determine our true heritage. Although some of the projects seemed unconventional, everyone gained a clearer understanding of the identity of self.

So what is identity? Basically, identity of self is the awareness of one's identity. Because I am conscious of myself, I am aware of my identity. From that understanding, I can perceive who I am and expand on my identity.

Although several aspects of identity, such as genetics and physical traits, are present at birth, many other important characteristics of identity develop over time. One important factor, changing and developing over an individual's lifetime, is the perception of self. A child's comprehension of his or her identity begins very simplistically, but grows much more complex in adulthood. According to Angela Oswalt, in one of her articles on *MentalHelp.net,* children first define their identities in the "Categorical Self," in which they describe themselves by attributes such as how old they are, what they look like, and their preferences. For example, a toddler might describe herself by her age, favorite color, and favorite toys. Oswalt notes that there are many influences on children's development of their identities and "both internal and external variables can affect young children's self-concept." In other words, how a child personally thinks and acts as well as the actions of others around the child will affect his or her understanding of identity.

Soon into the semester, I discovered the many different aspects that affect the development of self and personal identity. According to Hallel Mujingila Diakalenga in her article, *What Makes Up Our Identity,* "Identity is not formed based on only one source, which means that one must often draw upon multiple sources." Some of the main characteristics that influence identity are age, gender, physical features, race, heritage, beliefs, culture, and occupation. Each of those characteristics influences self in a different way. For example, I realized that race and heritage affect how an individual relates to his or her family and home. Meanwhile, beliefs and cultural norms can prompt how someone responds within a society or group. For instance, a Canadian woman of Asian descent may act and think very differently from a Jewish man living in the Netherlands. The way people associate themselves with others—friends, family, and even adversaries—affects their identities. Consider how family can influence an individual through commonly held customs, traditions, and beliefs. Friends and adversaries also shape a person's ideas in a positive or negative way. For example, a young woman may have been raised in a staunchly democratic home, but outside influences might sway her to consider the more conservative side of the Republican party. All these factors influence a person's identity.

Even though there are many elements that impact the development of an individual's identity, the personal perceptions an individual has of his or her identity is the crucial part that defines who a person is. Commonly, perceptions of self determine how someone comprehends information and how he or she will react in different situations. For example, a young man may think that he is very skilled in the fields of science and mathematics. Because of his perception, he may pursue a career as an engineer or professor of science. Essentially, individuals comprehend the world around them and then, from their perceptions of themselves and their environment, act in response to that.

However, there is often dissonance between the actual self and the perceived self. In a way, people see themselves and things around them through a personal lens—a perception filter, so to speak. This can have a dramatic impact on personal identity. Consider again the young man who sees himself as a skillful mathematician and scientist even though he has no talent in these subjects at all. How could he conclude that he is good at math and science when he is not? This is where the other aspects of identity come into play. He may be an exceptional test-taker, so his fantasy of being a scientist is based on results of other skills. Thus, the boy's success in the field of science depends on his ability to ace tests instead of his knowledge of science. However, it is also possible that this young man's father is a renowned scientist; thus, the boy believes that he will inherently be a great scientist as well. The perceived self and the actual self blend to form the identity of the individual. In the case of the hopeful scientist, the boy is really an academically intelligent individual who, although not excelling, enjoys studying science and math. Because his perceived self is a talented scientist, he may put in the effort to actually become a scientist.

Even though all people will have some incongruity between their actual and perceived selves, sometimes the imbalance is so great that it can result in serious problems. Often, this imbalance plays a large part in mental illnesses such as multiple personality disorder, depersonalization disorder, and dissociative amnesia. Most commonly, these illnesses are a defense for distressed or abused individuals and "are characterized by an involuntary escape from reality characterized by a disconnection between thoughts, identity, consciousness and memory" ("Dissociative"). In these cases, the identity of the individual is drastically distorted. For example, someone suffering multiple personality disorder has not one sole identity, but many different selves. The personal perception of his or her identity changes as the alternate personalities switch. Meanwhile, people who have depersonalization disorder suffer from "ongoing feelings of detachment from actions, feelings, thoughts and sensations as if they are watching a movie (depersonalization)" ("Dissociative"). Because of the illness, individuals' perception of the world around them is misconstrued.

Undoubtedly, I found this information about identity to be quite valuable. Of course, I had not felt this way at the start of the semester. When I first discovered what the class would be studying over the semester, I thought something like, "Identity should not be too difficult. After all, my identity is who I am, and I am myself. Honestly, this sounds rather uninteresting." Obviously, I was in for quite a surprise. What I believed would be a dull study on what it is like to be oneself, turned out to be research on much more complex aspects of the self. I had never fully contemplated how someone's culture and heritage differ, and how each affect that individual's identity. I found it astounding how an identity is not based on one single attribute, but is built on many layers of different characteristics that begin to develop in early childhood. Also, I thought it was positively chilling to consider

how the special and very complex identity of a person can be damaged
or altered by mental illnesses.

Naturally, everyone in the class has found a different feature about
identity that stands out to them, but what I find most important about
the identity of self is perception and how an individual perceives his or
her identity alters every other part of who they are. The perceptions
that people believe about themselves influence how they act each day,
and that in turn affects who they are which consequently shapes how
they perceive themselves. It is a cycle. Because the perceptions
someone has affects his or her identity, the perceptions of identity
essentially are what creates the individual's identity. For example, a
very uncoordinated girl firmly believes that she has the ability to
become a professional dancer. Her perceived self is the idea that she
has the raw talent to be a ballerina, while her actual self can hardly walk
in a straight line. The girl's identity is that of a naïve young dancer,
who cannot dance. Now, her perceived identity can change this
situation. Because she believes that she can become a ballerina, she
may work very hard and gradually gain the skills to become a dancer.
In this instance, her perceived self influenced her actions, which led to
her actual self being congruent with who she believed she was all along.
However, this result does not always occur. Perhaps the girl perceives
that she can dance, but after several years of trying without success, she
may decide that designing dance costumes is something she would
rather pursue. Her actual abilities and the influences around her caused
her to reconsider what she enjoys most about dance production. In
this case, her perception shifted. As a result, the girl realized that she

loves making the tutus more than wearing them herself, and her self-perception became more compatible with her actual skills.

To further elaborate, consider my own personal identity. From the fundamental, descriptive basis, I am a five-foot-tall, nineteen-year-old female, with brown hair and gray-blue eyes. Looking at my identity in the context of heritage, I am a citizen of the United States who was born in North Carolina and grew up in Missouri. Supposedly, my ancestors came from Wales and the Netherlands. And to define my identity by my roles and occupation, I am a Christian, daughter, sister, friend, music teacher, musician, composer, children's book illustrator, cartoonist, hunter, student at Ozarks Technical Community College, student in the OTC Honors program, and member of Phi Theta Kappa Honor Society. Examining who I am by my beliefs, I believe in the God of the Bible. By taking the Bible in context, I believe that there is absolute right and wrong, a rescue from personal wrongdoings by God, and an afterlife. I believe that every life is important and that men and women have very different but very important roles. And I firmly support hard work, perseverance, and honesty. Finally, to look at my identity by my personality, I am outgoing, sarcastic, determined, and easily excited. I love meeting people, being outdoors, and discovering new things. All these random things make up my identity.

However, before taking the English class, I never thought about how each different characteristic of myself combines to form my unique identity. Now, however, I realize that how I perceive myself is the core that defines my identity. For example, I proudly stated that I am a determined individual. That is how I see myself, ready to take on a task and stick with it until the job is done. Although my friends and family may say that this is certainly an attribute that I possess, they might also point out that my determination is more often manifested as stubbornness. Understanding this fact, I alter my perception of myself and separate my determination from my stubbornness. Thus, my new self-perception changes who I am and how I will act in future situations. Until the class study on identity, I had not realized how important it is to consider if how I perceive myself and how others see me is actually who I am.

Naturally, some might wonder, "All this information is fascinating, but why is understanding what identity is and how our perceptions alter our identities so important?" Certainly, this question is not without merit. After all, as an average individual, I probably will never need to know how the psychology of the actual and perceived identity relate— or do I? How I think about myself influences how I act. My actions affect others. If I perceive that I am a determined writer, even though I believe that my writing is very poor, I will try harder and strive to enhance my work. This will result in my writing being of a higher caliber and thus more influential to others. By understanding my perception of myself and wanting to change, I was able to improve myself and reach out more effectively to my readers.

However, there is more than just improving personal identity at stake. By not considering if personal perceptions of self are accurate, there can be dire consequences. Consider that a young man perceives himself as a careful and defensive driver. However, suppose that all his family and close friends warn him that he is often an irresponsible and careless driver when he is in a hurry. Outside influences encourage him to reevaluate his self-perception. But if he ignores that warning, his faulty view of himself could be disastrous—a car accident. That is only one example showing the results that individuals' perceptions of themselves can have impacting results on their lives. How people perceive their identity determines the way that they act, think, make decisions, treat others, work, believe, and raise the next generation. The actions, based on personal perceptions, of one person does not affect that individual alone. Those actions can impact a few people or everyone in the world.

Therefore, understanding identity is much more than just an interesting subject for an English class to study or even a good reason to travel the world on an expedition to find oneself. Knowing how we perceive ourselves affects every decision we make and every action we do. People are basically who they perceive themselves to be. But if individuals' perception is not true with how they react in situations or what the individuals actually can do, then it is vital that they rethink how they perceive themselves. Unlike the old saying, "You are what you eat," I believe that we are what we perceive. Therefore, we must look closely at what we think we see.

Works Cited

Diakalenga, Hallel. "What Makes Up Our Identity." *Odyssey*, 21 Aug.
    2016, https://www.theodysseyonline.com/what-makes-our-
    identity. 12 Apr. 2017.

"Dissociative Disorders." *National Alliance on Mental Illness*, n.d.,
    http://www.nami.org/ Learn-More/Mental-Health-
    Conditions/Dissociative-Disorders.

Oswalt, Angela. "Early Childhood Emotional and Social Development:
    Identity and Self-Esteem." *MentalHelp.net*, 16 Jan. 2008,
    https://www.mentalhelp.net/articles/early-childhood-
    emotional-and-social-development-identity-and-self-esteem/.
    10 Apr.

Ingredients for Identity

Viktoriia Hryshchenko

What makes a person's identity? You may have heard the phrases, "You act like your father" or "You take after your mother." Do these phrases lead us to believe your family dictates your identity? Scientists have made progressive research in DNA. Scientists can offer your choice of hair color, eye color, and height during the process of creating a baby, but can identity be the product of DNA? I believe a person's identity, my identity, is a combination of many things. I look at identity like a borscht, a famous soup from the Ukraine, where I am from. Every good soup starts with your base, in this case DNA. But there's more to it.

DNA is the foundation for what makes us who we are. Pork broth is the base for borscht, not the completed meal. We need ingredients to make it. With borscht, there are common ingredients almost everyone uses. This is no different than someone's identity. With that said, common ingredients for a person's identity include family, friends, church, and school. Now we are cooking. Each person's borscht is different. There are things added that are not found in every house. We add a little society and culture to the mix and we start having a product almost worth serving. To complete this meal, we need one more thing. The thing that makes every borscht fantastic—the secret ingredient. In the case of identity, the secret ingredient is freedom of choice. The freedom of choice is what takes the rest of the ingredients and decides which flavors it wants to enhance and which ones it will cancel out. Our identity is what makes us who we are. Not everyone will like your flavor, but it is your own unique recipe.

Let's start with our base. DNA or (deoxyribonucleic acid) is the main ingredient of life. Bill Gates states, "DNA is like a computer program but far, far more advanced than any software ever created" (228). DNA decides if we are born an elephant, frog, or human. Our DNA is around 99.5% the same as everyone else's on the planet, but it's that .5% that makes us different from the rest of the humans and starts giving us our own identity. Our DNA will decide our gender, hair color, eye color, height, race, and other physical characteristics. DNA is a combination of building blocks from our parents, but we can inherit DNA from other relatives, like grandparents, or great grandparents.

I would like to tell you that our relatives are the only deciding factor when it comes to DNA, but like food we have naturally grown ingredients and we have food that is artificial. Scientists have now found a way to artificially install specific genes into people's DNA to give them red hair, blue eyes, to make them tall, or even remove inherent flaws. I can understand the convenience of going to the grocery store and picking up a premade soup, but personally I like to make it myself and to ensure it's my own family recipe. With designer DNA, we have no idea what the lasting effects could be. The DNA could break down faster, or it could develop new diseases that humanity isn't ready for. What would happen if a designer human had offspring with non-designer humans? This doesn't even bring into account the ethics involved in this process. Where do we draw the line as a society when it comes to "playing God"? Currently, there is a strong debate amongst scientists on whether designer babies are ethical. Professor Sheldon Krimsky, from Tufts University, spoke about an upcoming trial on genetically engineering babies. He said, "It is unimaginable that any humane society would permit such a trial, where the potential risks so outweigh the social benefits" (Gallagher). This debate goes back and forth, and the questions have yet to be answered. It is safe to say in most countries genetic engineering of humans is illegal. We must continue to safeguard what makes us human and gives us our identity.

Now that we have the base we need the common ingredients that add to our identity. The first is family. Family has a lot to do with identity. It can influence politics, religion, occupational choices, language, and much more. These are the common things that can be on the surface of our identity or run deep and hidden. Families can influence a person's self-esteem, motivation level, confidence, and developmental skill sets. Let me give you a few examples. One is a parent who takes care of their child's every need, cleans, cooks, and lays out clothes. The parent taking complete care of his or her child can be seen as a nurturer. With that said, what are they teaching the child? What personality traits will the child gain for their identity?

Well, we can guess and say the child might be lazy. He or she may lack fundamental skills such as cooking or cleaning. The child might

not ever be able to function on his own. It teaches a person to be
dependent on others.

On the other hand, you have a parent who makes schedules,
instructs the child how to cook dinner, wash clothes, and contribute to
the household. This may lead us to believe the child will grow up more
independent and be a person that will function well on a team. There
are other things that can be a little more hidden. Children who grow
up mentally or physically abused may become isolated, violent, or have
no self-esteem. Family psychology and the part it plays on a person's
personality is a book by itself or many, many books for that matter, but
I think we understand the point of this ingredient.

What about friends? Like many other factors, friends can have a
big effect on our personality and how we approach things. According
to psychologist Steve DeBerry, "We tend to like and become friends
with people most similar to ourselves." If we tend to be friends with
people like ourselves how could it shape or change us? Just because
people are similar, it doesn't mean they are the same. Remember that
.5% with the DNA? I am sure there is a bigger percentage of
difference with people's personalities. Friends will have ideas,
behaviors, and attributes that we don't. With a person's desire to fit in,
we may adjust and learn to like the things our friends do. This can be a
more drastic adjustment or move for a boyfriend or girlfriend. With
that said, these new avenues that are different than our family will
shape our identities further.

For example, growing up I use to fear roller coasters. I remember
going to a festival with my friends in Kiev (a large city in Ukraine) and
seeing a roller coaster with turns and loops. I was terrified of going on

that ride. My friends Sasha and Kateryna begged me to go on the ride like a child pestering their parents for candy at the store. After about fifteen minutes of convincing I deferred to their wishes. As I climbed into the seat and the metal bar locked my body into place my heart sank. I instantly regretted giving into my friends' demands. The ride took off like a bullet and sent me back into my seat, and my heart began to race. A smile made its formation across my face because of this feeling of excitement. Since that day, I love roller coasters. One of my goals now is to ride every roller coaster in the United States. This is just one of the ways friends can shape your identity.

Church can also be a strong ingredient. Many people choose not to discuss church and have a tendency to be sweet or bitter depending on the person. But it is the thing that stays in the family or with others that use the same ingredient. McKenzie Smith says, "An individual's views on many topics may be dictated or decided by their religion, and more directly the religious community in which they participate" (Smith). The church's influence over a person's overall identity may depend on how involved they are with the church. A Buddhist monk may take a vow of silence or refrain from hurting any lifeform, while a member of Westboro Baptist church may teach their members to hate homosexuals or soldiers. Regardless of the religion it can have a big influence on how one thinks about the world. It can influence people's interactions with others, their beliefs, values, and even morals.

The last of the common ingredients is school. School is a combined seasoning, like *herbes de provence* (savory, marjoram, rosemary, thyme, oregano, and lavender). It has a little bit of everything mixed in, just like school. Schools have teachers, principals, counselors, friends, enemies, kitchen staff, janitors, and security. Some schools even have religious practices, although more uncommon in the United States. This has one of the biggest influences on how we develop our identities, and it seems to evolve and change the most during this time. Teachers can mold our minds like clay and instruct us on how we learn and what we learn when it comes to school. The principals set the rules for the school that we must follow, and they are enforced by security. The kitchen staff decide what we eat. Janitors clean and make changes to our environment. Our friends influence what we wear and who we like. Our enemies can add intimidation, resentment, or hate to our daily lives. Lastly, the counselors, help us decide our path after we leave school. This ingredient many times can make or break a dish. Our identity is at its most vulnerable during our high school years. Robert J. Hedya noticed, "One of the important things to remember is that what a teen does and is exposed to during this critical time in life, has a large influence on the teen's future, because experience and current needs shape the pruning and sprouting process in the brain."

Next, we move to the more uncommon ingredients. Society, and culture all play a part in how our identities develop into the final product. Society and culture are a very in-depth topic when it comes to how people develop. Society in its simplest form, as it described in Oxford Dictionary, "is a group of people involved in persistent social interaction, or a large social grouping sharing the same geographical or social territory, typically subject to the same political authority and dominant cultural expectations". To avoid being isolated in life we rely on fitting in with society. Society makes rules and customs that bring us all together towards a peaceful coexistence. As Thomas Jefferson said, "What is true of every member of the society, individually, is true of them all collectively; since the rights of the whole can be no more than the sum of the rights of the individuals." Society wants uniformity in the way we behave and act. Moreover, E.B. Tylor assumes, "Culture is that complex whole which includes knowledge, belief, art, morals, law, custom and any other capabilities and habits acquired by man as a member of society" (Taylor). I know it seems like society and culture can be the "end all be all" when it comes to individual identity. But this is not true; we have one more ingredient, the secret ingredient of freedom of choice.

The fundamental ingredient that makes us human and individuals is freedom of choice. Freedom of choice is what completes our identity. It is the one influence in how we develop that is all our own. Our parents, teachers, friends, church, or even society can influence us in many ways, but they cannot make that final choice for us. They can show us what they believe to be the best fit for us, what we should like, how we should act, or even what to think. This doesn't mean it's how the dish will come together. It is up to us as human beings, as individuals, to make the final decision on whether or not we like the Big Bang Theory (the television show, not the scientific theory…well, I guess that too.), whether or not we are pro-life or pro-choice, or like the color blue.

All these decisions can be influenced but not set in stone until we make that choice. I myself like having blue hair. My parents may not agree, society may frown on me standing out, my DNA did not give me blue hair, but I decided to have blue hair because of freedom of choice. It is my own secret ingredient that completes who I am. It makes me unique and different from everyone else. Identity means that you are your own unique individual. I firmly believe that if we laid out everything from my life starting with DNA and ending with freedom of choice, there will be no doubt that it could only be me. No other person would be identical to me.

In conclusion, what makes a person's identity? It's a combination of a good base, ingredients you find inside the house, some that come from the local area, and the secret ingredient of choice. The recipe for identities are not the same from person to person. We all have a little more or less of somethings and leave out others all together. Our recipe is our own and it's what makes us who we are. With that being said, I am going to include my recipe for borscht. I challenge you to give it a try, but I think even with my recipe you may change a few things to make it your own.

My Recipe for Borscht

Ingredients

- 1 pound beets (about 2 large beets)
- 1 large carrot, halved lengthwise and thinly sliced
- 1 pound of pork meat
- 2 potatoes
- 1 large onion, finely chopped
- Cabbage ½ pound, thinly chopped
- Bay leaf

- 1 pepper
- 2 tablespoons tomato paste
- Salt and pepper/ borscht spices
- 1 tablespoon chopped fresh dill
- 1/4 cup sour cream

How to put it all together:

1. Make a base or so-called bouillon from the pork meat by boiling it for a half an hour. Get rid of the white foam as soon as it appears on the bouillon's surface.
2. In a pan fry carrot, onion, potatoes, and pepper adding a little bit of sunflower oil. Take from the stove after a couple of minutes.
3. Put the mix of fried carrot, onion, potatoes, and pepper into the bouillon. (You can put onions by the end of making borscht, however, by putting it in the beginning, it has time to dissolve and will have a nice onion taste without actual onion's pieces)
4. While it is cooking, take another pan and fry cabbage, repeat and do the same with beets, until the pan will get red-pinkish color. It is better to fry them on separate pans, so the cabbage will have better taste.
5. Reduce heat to medium, add cabbage and beets to pan and cook, stirring often, until vegetables have softened, about 15 minutes. Add a bay leaf, bring the borsht to a boil over high heat; cover, reduce heat to low and simmer for 30 minutes. Stir

in tomato paste. Cook, uncovered, stirring occasionally, until all vegetables are very tender, about 15 minutes. Season with salt and pepper or borsht spices.

6. Fill a bowl with the borscht and top with scoop of sour cream and fresh dill just before serving.

Works Cited

DeBerry, Steve. "How Can Someone's Friends Affect Their Personality?" *How Can Someone's Friends Affect Their Personality?* Quora, 10 Feb. 2016. Web. 20 Apr. 2017.

Gallagher, James. "'Designer Babies' Debate Should Start, Scientists Say." *BBC News*. BBC, 19 Jan. 2015. Web. 7 May 2017.

Gates, Bill "The Road Ahead." *Penguin Readers*. London, Revised, 1996 p. 228

Hedaya, Robert J. "The Teenager's Brain." *Psychology Today*. Sussex Publishers, 03 June 2010. Web. 20 Apr. 2017.

"The Papers of Thomas Jefferson." *The Founders' Constitution*. Volume 1, Chapter 2, Document 23. Edited by Julian P. Boyd et al. Princeton: Princeton University Press, 1950.

Tylor, Edward Burnett. "Researches Into the Development of Mythology, Philosophy, Religion, Art, and Custom". *Primitive Culture*. Vol.1, 1871.

"Why Are the Genomes of Humans 99.5% the Same?" *Biology Stack Exchange*. N.p., n.d. Web. 20 Apr. 2017.

How the Environment We Grew Up in Can Affect Our Identity as Adults

Olivia Meyers

Freshman year of high school is a significant year for most people, but I moved halfway across the country to a new environment filled with new people, a new school, and new experiences. Moving from Pennsylvania to Missouri at fifteen was a big change for me, and it helped make me who I am today. From the food we eat, to the hobbies we have and even the friends we keep, our personalities stem from the environment we grew up in and whether we realize it or not, our family, our geography, and the relationships we make have an impact on our identities.

To begin, family is a topic that is close to everyone's heart because it is the people that we have been surrounded by since before we can remember. Whether it was biological family or the people we relate to as family, all the same, they are the first relationships that we have ever formed and our first means of learning how to share, communicate and interact with others. I would say our family environment has a huge influence on who we become as people because they are the first people we may admire and pay attention to; family is essentially the first model we have for how to act and be as a grown up and person in general. By stating this, I mean that we may learn our beliefs, point of views, interests, and traditions from our family. Author Philip Wittmeyer makes an interesting point about this in his article, "Family Influence":

> [O]ur parents taught us all the basics of "proper" behavior. When we were small children, we jolly well did whatever impulse entered our heads. We did not know that it was socially unacceptable to eat with our fingers, to play with the vase on the coffee table, to hit our brother, to break our toys. These and a million other rules were drummed into our heads by our parents. (Wittmeyer)

The examples that Wittmeyer gives are impulses that our parental figures have taught us to avoid. There are many examples of things that we have learned from our families that simply come naturally to us now such as the way we use a fork, or put the left shoe on the left foot and right shoe on the right foot. It is just normal to us the way we make certain foods and why we are more biased towards one thing rather than another. These and a multitude of other everyday choices that we make without putting too much thought into them are influenced by our family. Our preferences have been impacted by our family dynamics, socioeconomic level, and the opportunities that were available to us.

Family dynamic has an impact on our lives because it is how we developed our skills of communication with others. This impact is defined by counselor and psychotherapist Joshua Miles as "the patterns and interactions we have with different members of our family. Each family has a unique set of dynamics, which will impact our development, ideas, and ways of behaving as well as how we interact with others" (Miles). So these dynamics would be things like the way we ask permission from our parents to do things, the way we ask for help on things from siblings, or even how we have certain understandings between the family like how parents sit at the head of the table or how one sibling is trusted to help with the youngest. Another way family dynamics can be looked at is the difference in families such as being an adopted child, living with grandparents or cousins, or even having a blended family. Family dynamics differ in every situation and therefore affect everyone, presently and later in life in different ways. In other words, if someone has to become a responsible sibling at a young age that would definitely impact their sense of independence and trust of others as they grow up. Another example of this would be if a family has strong values and teaches this to their children, such as if one is taught to be a go-getter, these family values would easily impact the confidence of a growing child and how they see themselves, whether they embrace that family value or reject it. Family dynamics can also change one's views of relationships later in life; I would say that one's home life and who they live with growing up influences their identity later in life because it would change one's level of respect, helpfulness, courtesy, manners and a multitude of other aspects of personality one may take for granted.

The other aspect of a person's family life that can influence their identity later in life is a family's socioeconomic level which coincides with the opportunities available to person. The Journal of

Marriage and the Family U.S. National Library of Medicine makes this clear:

> [T]he economic decline during the last decade has placed significant pressures on many families in terms of financial distress, reduced employment opportunities, and fewer resources to help family members pursue their educational goals…. [T]hese dimensions of economic, occupational, and educational experience represent important markers of social class or socioeconomic status. (Conger and Martin)

Family economics hold importance because they are involved in the amount of time parents can give to their child, the amount of stress on the family to make ends meet, the opportunities available to a child and, in the end, all this adds up to affect the identity of a child in their adult life. The reason why economics affect the amount of time parents can give to their children is because if a parent is working three jobs to be able to keep a roof over the family's head it is going to absolutely take away from the amount of time that that parent can allot to family time because there simply are not enough hours in a day. If we were to compare this to a family that is a bit more economically stable, the parents in the latter of the two would most likely have more time to spend helping with homework or doing family activities together. The reason why this influences a person's identity is because children can feel the stress their parents may be going through and it can make a child wonder whether school is more important than getting a job and helping at home.

I have seen this first hand because I watched my sister practically work full time and finish high school to help my mother, a single parent at the time, pay the bills. Watching parents struggle and working to help out can affect one's work ethic and their feelings toward money later in life when they are gaining it themselves from watching their family struggle or living life more carefree. In my case, my family's financial level has fluctuated over time from a single mother household to the addition of my stepdad and our blended family. As one can imagine that the difference in income modified the amount of family time and opportunities I had available to me growing up. Coming to maturity in a situation like this has also given me a lot of respect for my elders and the things that they do and have done for me because I have witnessed that struggle, firsthand, from my mom trying please everyone, be both parents and find the time for herself.

Furthermore, economics in the family definitely matter because they influence the opportunities available to the children such as after school opportunities, school trips, summer events, and going to a college institution later in their school careers. Missing out on these events, due to reasons such as not having the money to afford them, can deeply impact a child because these are opportunities that help expand a child's mind, help build communication skills among peers and, more obviously, missing out on a college education can change their career goals and affect their own families later in life when it comes to personal expenses. A child's home environment easily influences a growing identity because of the family relationships, socioeconomic level and what opportunities are available to them.

The second element of environment that influences one's identity is the actual area one grew up in meaning, comparatively, the city or country, the East coast to West coast, the North compared to the

South, and Midwest. Living in a different area affects one's personality because, again, of the opportunities and what is available. Accordingly, in my experience, in Pennsylvania there is the beach, there are big cities, history and a multitude of food that was prevalent in that area which is much different than the state of Missouri. Here, we have lakes, small cities, different aspects of history and food favorites that are more southern oriented than one would expect to find on the Coast. Author of *Place-Identity: Physical World Socialization of the the Self,* Harold M. Proshansky, supports this idea that the location of where one grew up at is relevant in personality by defining place identity as, "a substructure of self-identity consisting of memories, ideas, feelings, attitudes, values, preferences, meanings, and conceptions of behavior and experience that occur in places that satisfy an individual's biological, psychological, social, and cultural needs" (Proshansky, Fabian and Kaminoff). I would agree with Proshansky's definition because I think it is true that place identity is something we all experience with our home town/state/location. For example, I would include Pennsylvania as part of my place identity because it is included in my personality such as the way my East Coast accent comes out, my taste in foods, my comfort for living in the fast-pace city, and even in the way I view politics since I have more of an open mind from living in a more diverse place like the East coast. These parts of my identity are different than from what I have acquired from living in Missouri which would include things like the way I enjoy being outdoors and have found my passion for animals that will one day affect my career choice. I would say that the differences in these areas have influenced my identity because I didn't realize the change in states would create such a contrast in activities and social norms, but I have learned to adjust to the difference.

To continue, social norms are to be included because they also affect identity in ways that differ from where one grew up at as well. An article from the Journal of Behavioral Decision Making, titled "Do the Right Thing: But Only if Others Do So" states that social norms "…ought to be understood as a kind of grammar of social interactions. Like a grammar, a system of norms specifies what is acceptable and what is not in a society or group." This definition is explaining is that social norms are something that are just accepted in society as common qualities of the people in that community. Therefore, social norms can change from place to place because different locations have different customs.

For example, in a big city it is normal not to have a car and to just take a taxi somewhere or walk compared to living in the country where most people may have a truck and own land for farming. Social norms can also be things like the demographic of people in the area and the type of outfits people may wear. I a bigger metropolitan area it can be seen to have more of a diverse culture with people wearing things that are a bit more risqué than what one might see in a small town. There we might find that a lot of the community know each other, like family, and dress more concentionally than in the city. One thing to note about social norms is that they fit into our society without our knowledge like an expected decency of people. Social norms can affect the identity of a person because they would be what they have come to expect of the world such as living in a high poverty area where the people in this area may be convinced that it is difficult to move out of this situation. Another example of social norms being an unacknowledged aspect of a community would be like living in California and seeing famous actors in casual places doing everyday things like getting coffee. In my experience, when I moved to Nixa, Missouri it was just accepted that most teenagers had a decent car that their parents paid for, whereas in Pennsylvania high schoolers had a car that they worked for themselves. I would say that social norms affect our identity because they are what we come to expect of the world without too much explanation, whereas someone who is from a different place than ourselves would view doing something like standing in line for coffee with Jerry Seinfeld to be unheard of. It can be concluded that the geographical environment that we grow up in affects our identity from the way that places differ and what social norms are customary to the place because different areas have different traditions and values that shape our identities.

The final reason that environment affects our identity is that the people in our everyday environment such as at school and work also impact our identity. To start, our earliest relationships with people besides our families was in school with our classmates and eventual friends. Counseling article "Peer Relationships and Identity" reads, "The impact of peers on adolescents cannot be underestimated. The right people crossing their path at critical times can reinforce positive values and enhance the entire process of growing up. The wrong individuals can escort them into extremely negative detours or suck the life out of them" (Focus on the Family). Accordingly, making these relationships as we're growing up with our peers has serious impact on our personalities because they can influence who we become as people.

The friends that we grow up with leave an impression on our identity because they are the first formation of relationships outside the family and so we may place importance on their opinions and actions. This can lead to doing similar activities, agreeing with the things they may say or do and potentially becoming a follower in another's footsteps all of which can have good and bad consequences.

For instance, if we were to, at a young age, befriend someone with a good work ethic and goals then we may be more inclined to have these same qualities. Conversely, if we were to befriend someone who has the tendency to slack off on responsibilities then it is possible that this could affect our personalities too and that could leave a negative impact on our personality. Personally, I remember growing up with friends that had more easy-going parents than my own and this lead me to have some bad/learning experiences such as sneaking out but I also made friends that turned me around and made me see the importance of goals. Influence from friends can then lead into the subject of confidence because our peers can make or break that characteristic in our personalities due to the fact that we place importance on our peer's opinions. Having confidence in our identities matters because it coincides with our self-esteem and when one does not have confidence it can lead to difficulty making decisions, engaging in unhealthy relationships and more serious issues such as depression, anxiety, eating disorders and addictions (Musby). Thus, our everyday relationships that we make growing up have an impact on our identities, possibly more than we realize, because of their likeliness to influence our personal psychological views.

Also, another aspect that is important to include in our environment that involves our relationships is the amygdala, a tiny part of our brain responsible for emotions such as anger, fear, sadness and aggression. It works to store memories of events and emotions so that one may be able to recognize and react to what seems like a similar situation later (Williams). This part of the brain is necessary to mention when talking about identity because its function is something that comes out in our identity without our knowing through the relationships that we have made. Furthermore, the motive for mentioning the amygdala is to trace it back to bullying. Over 3.2 million students are victims of bullying each year (Cohn) and I would conclude that that fear and state of depression that bullying brings out in a child are emotions that stay and affects that child's personality later in life. In my personal experience, it certainly did. I moved around a lot in school and in sixth grade I was that kid that got mocked, criticized, and teased for just about everything I did by everyone in the class and I never understood why. I tried my best to be nice to everyone at every new school I attended. However, after that I moved to a new school, made a few friends, and then a couple years later, we moved to Missouri to start it all over again. By that time, I decided to just keep my head above water and get through the rest of my high school years looking out for myself because, after being bullied and moving around so much, I was simply tired of putting on an act for people I may never see again and honestly had no personal ties to. I'll even make the claim that my amygdala came into play and is the reason why I never bounced back into trying to be good to everyone and just kept mainly to myself instead of going through the process of making new connections that would soon be dismissed as well. I would say that the amygdala coincides with our environment and relationships because it remembers past experiences and shows the effects of those events in our personality and the way we react to similar situations later on.

Oscar Wilde once said, "Most people are other people. Their thoughts are someone else's opinions, their lives a mimicry, their passions a quotation." In conclusion, I would say that what we perceive as our identity is the things that we gather through our environment similarly to what Mr. Wilde has stated. Things like what food we enjoy, our accent, the opinions we keep, the mindset that we have and a multitude of other aspects of our personalities are all things that we have acquired through family, the location of where we grew up and the relationships that we have made from childhood. In my experience, I would say that the environment that we grow up in certainly affects our identity because the biggest adventure that happened to me, while coming of age, would be my move from Pennsylvania to Missouri my freshman year of high school.

Works Cited

Bicchieri, C. and E. Xiao (2009). "Do the right thing: but only if others do so," *Journal of Behavioral Decision Making*, 22: 191–208. Web. 20 Apr. 2017.

Cohn, Andrea, and Andrea Canter, Ph.D. "Bullying: Facts for Schools and Parents." NASP Fact Sheet. Web. 20 Apr. 2017.

Conger, Rand D., Katherine J. Conger, and Monica J. Martin. "Socioeconomic Status, Family Processes, and Individual Development." *Journal of Marriage and the Family. U.S. National Library of Medicine*, 1 June 2010. Web. 12 Apr. 2017.

Miles, Joshua. "Family Dynamics and the Roles We Play." *Counselling Directory*. N.p., 30 June 2015. Web. 10 Apr. 2017.

Musby, Eva, and Tabitha Farrar. "Identity and Self Esteem." *Mirror Mirror Eating Disorder Help*. N.p., n.d. Web. 20 Apr. 2017.

"Peer Relationships and Identity." *Focus on the Family*. The Complete Guide to Baby & Child Care, 06 May 2011. Web. 20 Apr. 2017.

Proshansky, Harold M., Abbe K. Fabian, and Robert Kaminoff. "Place-identity: Physical World Socialization of the Self." *The Journal of Environmental Psychology* 3.1 (1983): 57-83. Science Direct. Web. 12 Apr. 2017.

Williams, John. "The Amygdala: Definition, Role & Function." *Study.com*, n.d. Web. 20 Apr. 2017.

Wittmeyer, Philip. " Family Influence - Michael Teachings." *The Michael Teachings*, n.d. Web. 10 Apr. 2017.

The Science of Self
Lane Williamson

You are an individual. Nobody is exactly like you. Nobody has the same hair as you, the same nose as you, or that weird pain you get in your left leg when you stand up too fast. All of these things are what make you who you are. Being you means that you talk, feel, move, react, and perceive everything from a unique perspective that no one else can truly know. Was it some divine force that gave you all these qualities and showed you your true self? The complete answer has yet to be found, but there is significant evidence that points to our genetic make up being the source of who we are. You are born with a genetic code that creates every part of you, both mentally and physically. This means that every person is only unique in their DNA variation and past experiences.

First off, the genetic code that every single human on Earth has is DNA. DNA, or Deoxyribonucleic Acid, is the material that is passed down in humans to create new life ("What is DNA?"). DNA is made up of chemicals that create the code for every feature that makes you up ("What is DNA?"). DNA is the blueprint of what makes a living creature what it is. It basically stores all of the information on how to build the parts of your body and passes on that information to cells to do the actual building ("What is DNA?"). So every feature that you have was built using DNA. Your DNA is essentially a combined copy of your parents' DNA because it has the ability to replicate itself ("What is DNA?") So, the fact that you have the same features or tendencies as your parents or siblings is because of your similar DNA. It is the building block of all life and is what makes up who you are.

Furthermore, the reason why DNA is so important in determining that you are born your true self before any life experiences, is that your DNA contains all of the necessary information that you need to live. No matter what happens in your life, the information for how you react with things, how you look as you age, and how your personality will change is programmed in your DNA at birth.

Second, genetic variation is one of the main reasons why people differ as much as they do. Genetic variation is "a term used to describe the variation in the DNA sequence in each of our genomes. Genetic variation is what makes us all unique, whether in terms of hair colour, skin colour or even the shape of our faces" ("What is Genetic"). There are many instances in current society of genetic variation helping to improve the functionality of the human body and increase survival. A more obvious variation in society is color of skin. African humans usually have darker colored skin because it is a variant that allows them to keep their brains cool and protect their skin from UV radiation (Moan). Europeans adapted to an area with less harsh sunlight, so they have lighter skin to absorb more UV rays to receive their Vitamin D (Moan). This shows that the genetic variation between the people from two different areas adapted to help them survive and become more productive. Although genetic variation makes us look different and have different survival tools, we are all still built from mostly the same genetic material. More than ninety-nine percent of DNA is shared between all humans ("What is DNA?"). This means that a small one percent is what makes us differ as people.

Furthermore, genetic variation happens in many different areas of the body for survival and functionality purposes. The abstract from the book *Establishing, Maintaining and Modifying DNA Methylation Patterns in Plants and Animals* explains that we have already found many of the exact strands of DNA that correlate to certain physical and mental attributes, and have processes of replacing and repairing them (Law and Jacobsen). The process is not perfected, nor is every physical and mental attribute found in DNA, but research is headed in that direction very quickly. Genetic variation is just a scientific way of showing that the attributes found in your DNA that make you up differ only slightly from your peers' attributes. It helps to create individualism and ensure the survival of the human race, but with advancements in changing DNA manually, it is possible that people will soon be able to choose who they want their children to be. This would take the gambling portion out of having children, and if used correctly, could ensure the survival and healthiness of the human race indefinitely. By matching up the correct genes, you could potentially eliminate many conditions and diseases from your children, making them healthy.

Next, one thing that helps to classify an organism is the ability to react to stimuli in a surrounding environment. Stimuli is either an internal or external stimulus that triggers a sense to help the organism react to its environment and insure survival ("Living Organisms"). For instance, when your mouth gets dry, that is your body's stimuli telling you that you need to drink water. All people are born with the ability to react to stimuli because it is a characteristic of life ("Living Organisms"). The human brain remembers many stimuli throughout life, and sometimes marks them using emotions. This stimuli helps to define who you are because it can determine possible hobbies or things that you like to do. For example, if someone refuses to swim in a pool, it may be because they had a traumatic swimming incident as a child.

So, some individuals think that your past experiences help to change you to the person you are today, but that statement is only somewhat correct. Basically, what you have been through in life can change how you react to certain situations because of your memory and past stimuli. This does make up who you are as a person, but more in the scientific way of reacting to stimuli and storing information than the literal sense of the experiences. Stimuli is just another example of how your genetic makeup determines who you are from birth.

Another impact on who you become is how you are raised. Everything you do and everything your parents do when raising you are just examples of stimuli reactions and instructions in your DNA taking place in the brain that causes a person to react to the situation. Any decision that you make, or any person makes for that matter, is just a reaction that takes place in your brain. These decisions are made by basing information off of your DNA and past experiences. So being raised does impact who you become, but in no different way than any other person. It helps to form who you are as an individual, but still follows the same blueprint that everyone else does. You will become a different person based on the experiences you go through in life, but the setup and the chemicals behind it all is the same for every person.

It all comes down to the information that you are born with. Your DNA is the ultimate guide for who you are going to be as a person.

Next, intelligence, in the sense of logic and problem solving skills, is something that is very much tied to your genes. How intelligent you are definitely has an impact on who you truly are. Many researchers would argue that it is hard to prove that intelligence comes from genetics because even though families have similar IQs, they also usually have similar environments that they are raised in (Is Intelligence Determined). While this may be true that it would be hard to separate this study, intelligence goes further than an IQ test. It is the ability to learn and understand things. Even without something like an IQ test, intelligence can still be measured.

To further explain, every person is born with a certain degree of capabilities. The amount of intelligence that you have is programmed into your DNA. If your environment changes and that gives you access to more knowledge and resources, then it is already programmed in you how to handle that. So yes, your environment certainly changes the intelligence that you have in certain cultures or societies, but your true intelligence has been there since birth.

Finally, the soul is a very intriguing part of human life. The soul is something seen by many people in many ways, but is widely accepted to be something that gives the individual purpose, and is the location of the true self. Everything we do physically and mentally can be scientifically explained, but the soul cannot be. There are many theories out there but none with solid evidence that can confirm or deny a soul.

However, there is one theory that is somewhat firm on the exact origin of the soul. While the soul cannot be proven real with science, it could simply be something that humans created to cope with our overwhelming intelligence, as compared to other species, given to us by our DNA. It is how we evolved, and is nothing more than a mechanism that helps us keep our sanity by giving us comfort in a place to go after death. While this theory doesn't have much evidence supporting it to make it a fact, it is one of the more realistic ideas behind the soul. People like the feeling of positive emotions, and the soul is a way for them to direct those emotions into positive endings of life. While many people would consider the soul to be the center of who is your true self, others would say it is nothing but a man-made figment of thought.

While every person differs and is unique, it is not because they are special by some unknown force, but because of their DNA and how they react to stimuli. Each of the parts of your life are formed from these two things. While the hobbies you have and the friends you have may vary depending on your life experiences, the way you react with everything in life is already set in stone from the time you are born. Even though you are born with DNA and stimuli set in place to form you into the person that you will be, you can still enjoy it and make conscious decisions along the way. Every decision you make and every action you take is based completely off of your DNA and your stimuli reacting to life itself, thus forming who you truly are.

Works Cited

ESchooltoday. "Living Organisms Respond to Their Environment."
Living Organisms Respond to Their Environment, Eschooltoday, 20 Mar.
2017, Accessed 20 Mar. 2017.
eschooltoday.com/science/characteristics-of-living-
organisms/living-organisms-adapt-and-respond-to-their-
environment.html.

Law, Julie A., and Steven E. Jacobsen. "Establishing, Maintaining and
Modifying DNA Methylation Patterns in Plants and Animals."
Nature Reviews. Genetics, U.S. National Library of Medicine, 20 Mar.
2010, Accessed 22 Mar. 2017.
www.ncbi.nlm.nih.gov/pmc/articles/PMC3034103/.

Moan, Joan. "Why Skin Colours Differ." *Department of Physics*, UiO
Department of Physics, 15 Mar. 2011, Accessed 22 Mar. 2017.
www.mn.uio.no/fysikk/english/research/news-and-
events/news/2011/why-skin-colours-differ.html.

U.S. National Library of Medicine. "Is Intelligence Determined by
Genetics? - Genetics Home Reference." *U.S. National Library of
Medicine*, National Institutes of Health, 20 Mar. 2017, Accessed 20
Mar. 2017. ghr.nlm.nih.gov/primer/traits/intelligence.

U.S. National Library of Medicine. "What Is DNA? - Genetics Home
Reference." *U.S. National Library of Medicine*, National Institutes of
Health, 20 Mar. 2017, Accessed 20 Mar. 2017.
ghr.nlm.nih.gov/primer/basics/dna.

Yourgenome.org. "What Is Genetic Variation?" *Facts*, The Public
Engagement Team at the Wellcome Genome Campus, 4 Feb. 2015,

Accessed 20 Mar. 2017. www.yourgenome.org/facts/what-is-genetic-variation.

Intertwined

Kendra Caruso

Who are you? Are you just a genetic compilation of your parents? Am I simply a product of my raising? Are we all only a reflection of our experiences? Or do all of these things combine to make us who we are? I believe that like multi-colored threads woven together to create a rich and intricate ornate tapestry, our genetics and environments, are interwoven to form a rich and intricately ornate, multi-faceted personality. Our nature and our nurture interplay to form our identities, and all quite possibly remain malleable throughout our lifetimes.

As a science major (currently in biology and next psychology) I have long had an interest in these topics and have been fortunate enough to get the chance to further research and gain a deeper understanding of how these "threads" of DNA and experiences are woven together to create such a complex "tapestry" of one's self. Ideas and study results from biology and psychology offer insight into the nature vs. nurture debate, how they affect our identities, and whether we can alter the effects which nature and nurture have on our identities.

In a nutshell, our "nature" refers to our inherited genetics and DNA. Each of us receive half of our forty-six chromosomes from our father and the other half from our mother. These chromosomes are made up of strands of DNA that are made up of segments of code, or instructions for each cell, called a gene. It is common to think of each gene as functioning as a set of instructions for a certain trait (although there are exceptions), or set of characteristics, like eye color and shape, hair color and texture, and skin color and race. The entire set of instructions, or all of our genes, combined is called a genome. Every cell in our bodies contain strands of DNA that are tightly wrapped around proteins that act like a support structure called histones, like string wrapped around a spool. These histones, or "spools,"can be modified to open or close allowing different segments of genes to be accessed by molecules called silencing markers. These silencing markers can collect on the gene essentially turning it "off," or be removed essentially turning the gene "on." This process is called epigenetics and is affected by environmental factors which are a part of our "nurture" aspect, causing changes which alter the way a gene is expressed. This means that while our DNA stays the same, our "nurture" may alter the way our "nature" works.

"Nurture," in a nutshell, refers to our raising, our environments, and our experiences through life. Parents are a child's first teachers and often teach their children the alphabet, table manners, and how to tie their shoes. Parents can also unintentionally influence their children's fears (such a fear of spiders or heights) and even relationship dynamics (by watching mom and dad interact). Our raising is a combination of learning, influences, and relationships, that help shape identity, but it certainly does not end with our parents. Where we live, the kinds of schools and communities we are part of, and the people we are around greatly influence us and our behavior. The environments we are in can persuade many of our choices from what we eat to where we work. Our environments are a combination of our surroundings, diets, and even income levels. This can help determine the types of major life events we have (such as getting a degree or going to jail), and the way that we view and interact with the world around us. Our experiences are a combination of events, circumstances and perceptions, and these help to shape our identities. Nurture, personality traits, and identity are complex and are a combination of our raising, our environments, and our experiences through life. Much in the same way that a fine tapestry is woven with unique and intricate patterns, our lives are woven with unique experiences that help shape who we are.

Questions of who we are and how we became that way have been with us since humanity's beginnings. A thoughtful debate has been burning in many minds about this, commonly known as the "nature vs. nurture debate." This debate has been sparked with one simple question: is who we are a sum of our DNA *or* a sum of our experiences? Great minds have pondered this very question and the debate is rooted in ancient philosophy. Plato believed that who we are is entirely inherited from our parents, while Aristotle believed that who we are is entirely dependent on our environment and experiences. Later during the Enlightenment period, physician John Locke seemed to agree with the "nurture" side of this debate by explaining that we are all born with a "blank slate" and that our environment and raising completely decide who we become. The debate was reignited after

Charles Darwin's book, *On the Origin of Species*, was published describing evolution through natural selection, or in other words that we are our biology. Darwin's cousin, Francis Galton, began his own research looking further into inherited traits passed down from parent to child and coined the term "nature versus nurture." The debate raged on with many psychologists taking the "nurture" side of the debate.

Many twentieth-century psychologists developed their own take on the nurture theory. Among them was John Watson, known as the father of behaviorism, who believed that who we are and how we behave is product of our raising and environments. Today philosophy, psychology, and biology understand and agree that who we are, or our identities, are a combination of all the different factors that make up our nature and our nurture. With the completion of the Human Genome Project at the turn of this century, we now have a virtual map of all of a human's genes (or genome), in the correct order, which is being studied to find out how genetics, environments, and behavior affect each other. It seems that nature and nurture are intertwined and work *together* to make us who we are, and that the nature vs nurture debate has been doused. In other words, who we are is a sum of our DNA *and* a sum of our experiences.

Far from being a "blank slate," many modern psychologists hold that we are each born with a pre-programed base personality, or inborn temperament. There are three basic temperaments, defined by researchers Thomas and Chess in the 1950's, commonly known as "difficult babies," "slow to warm-up babies," and "easy babies." Difficult babies tend to resist new experiences and often have intense, negative reactions to things, while slow to warm-up babies tend to be a bit difficult at first but become easier over time. Easy babies tend to be open to new experiences and often have calm, cheerful reactions to things. This shows that we have an inborn, possibly inherited, base personality before we even draw our first breath.

As we get older, much of personal identity comes down to personality and behavior. This is measured by psychologists with a widely used and highly regarded tool called the Big Five personality test. It works by measuring an individual's ranges on a scale for each of these five main personality traits: openness, conscientiousness, extroversion, agreeableness, and neuroticism.

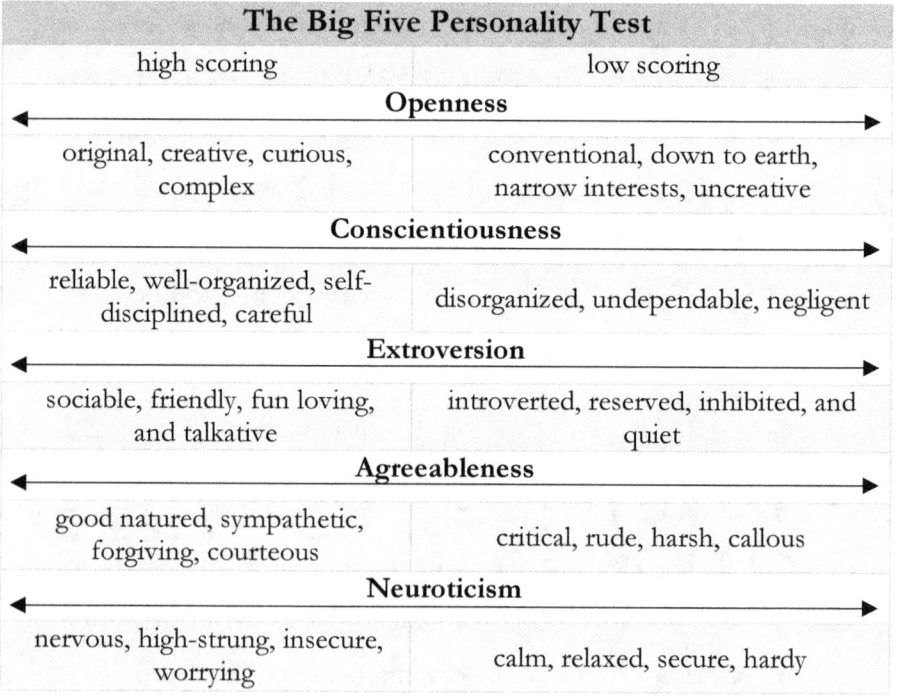

The Big Five Personality Test	
high scoring	low scoring
Openness	
original, creative, curious, complex	conventional, down to earth, narrow interests, uncreative
Conscientiousness	
reliable, well-organized, self-disciplined, careful	disorganized, undependable, negligent
Extroversion	
sociable, friendly, fun loving, and talkative	introverted, reserved, inhibited, and quiet
Agreeableness	
good natured, sympathetic, forgiving, courteous	critical, rude, harsh, callous
Neuroticism	
nervous, high-strung, insecure, worrying	calm, relaxed, secure, hardy

Because our nurture is so complex, this tool offers a way to measure our identities and attempt to analyze the effects that our environments, experiences, and raising have had in shaping who we become.

As children, we are especially attuned to learning from our environments, both through our own experiences and through the adult influences in our lives. Fear can be learned through personal experience, such as being bitten by a snake and consequently, becoming afraid of snakes. Fear can also be learned through influence, such as seeing your parents' fearful reaction to snakes and consequently fearing them yourself. These fears can extend from person to person, and can last a lifetime. In a classic experiment by John Watson in the 1920's a baby called "Little Albert" was used to test fear conditioning, or learned fear. At first, the baby enjoyed the white rat that he was shown, but when Watson paired the white rat with the banging of hammers hitting pipes, the baby became fearful and anxious. Through repetition of this experiment, "little Albert" began to generalize his new fear and cried at the sight of nearly anything white and fuzzy, from dogs to coats. This is an extreme case, in a controlled study (that would be considered unethical today), that helps to illustrate the way that fears can be easily learned, especially by young, easily influenced minds. Many of the things we learn and the experiences we have as children continue on with us into adulthood, and can help shape our identities and behaviors.

Similarly, relationship dynamics often seem to be learned through influence, simply by watching and mimicking the adults in our lives. In another classic experiment, this one in the 1960's by Albert Bandura, a "Bobo doll" was used to test children's responses to watching adult aggression. Each child was brought into a room with several toys including a "bobo doll," much like children's inflatable, sand-filled bottom punching bags on the market today. After the children had been playing for a bit, an adult would come into the room and begin to play alongside the child. In one group the adult would play calmly with the bobo doll, and in the other group the adult would begin to punch, throw, shout, and even use a toy hammer on the bobo doll. The children in the first group tended to play calmly and even speak kindly to the bobo doll when left alone to play again. However, the children in the second group began to abuse the bobo doll in the same manner as they had watched, and even used creativity in their own violence. This illustrates the way that as children we are influenced simply by watching and mimicking those around us.

Our early experiences, raising, and environments can have a lasting impact, both negatively and positively, on who we become as adults. A long term psychosocial study in 2014 found that (along with inherited base temperament and income levels), there is a strong link between home environments and future success. Children were observed from birth to 32 years old, and those who grew up in caring and supportive homes tended to later "score better on tests, get along better with peers, attain higher degrees, and were more satisfied in their romantic relationships" (Singh). The types of environments we grow up and spend our time in seem to have a large impact on our behaviors and personal identities for decades into our adulthood.

However, it is not only nurture that impacts who we are. An international study on "genome-wide associations" in 2016, shows a few specific gene segments have direct links to personality traits described by the Big Five test. This new research shows that the genes that are connected to these personality traits, when overlapped and compared, are the same genes that have previously been connected to specific mental disorders. In the 2016 study, links were found connecting genes in very high scorers in neuroticism with major depressive disorder and generalized anxiety disorder, just as links to high levels of openness correlated with schizophrenia and bipolar disorder. This held true as well for very high scores in extroversion which were frequently found with a diagnosis of with ADHD, although there were no disorders tied to high scores in agreeableness or conscientiousness. However, it is vital to stress that these "mental illnesses are largely inborn personality traits that get pushed into extreme territory by life experiences," rather than simply being a genetic destiny (Healy). Studies like this help confirm that nature and nurture are intertwined in the formation of identity. We come with a fixed set of inherited genetics and personality predispositions at birth, then beginning in childhood (and throughout life) our environments influence our behaviors and habits.

We now have the knowledge and technology that the great minds before us did not; we have learned many of the secrets of the human gene, examined the way it nudges our experiences in life through temperament and personality traits, and we have begun to unravel the mysterious interplay of epigenetics and environments. The big question now is can nature and nurture affect each other enough to be altered or modified by choice? Over the last decade several experiments have been run with a set of genetic clones (same "nature"), to see what would be different if they were to be raised separately (different "nurture"), and what (if anything) would be different if they were raised together (same "nurture"). When a fertilized egg splits in half, identical twins are later born, which gives us two individuals who are as close to being genetically identical as can be found outside of a science lab: (nearly) genetic clones.

Stories about identical twins, separated at birth and later reunited as adults, have become infamous. One of the most striking examples was from a 1979 study with a set of twins that had both "married women named Linda, divorced, and married the second time to women named Betty. One named his son James Allan, the other named his son James Alan, and both named their pet dogs Toy" (Than). These twins had never met, were raised in entirely different home environments, and had nothing else in common except their biology. Examples like these seem to clearly show similarities from internal factors: genetics.

However, as identical twin studies have been conducted over the past century, not all of the twins have been raised apart. Often used as a control rather than a test, these genetic clones were raised in the same home, producing two people with the same nature and the same nurture. Yet, surprisingly, there were some striking differences in these twins, particularly when it came to health. Despite the stories of twins giving their children and their pets the same names, researchers have noticed that identical twins often die years apart, from different diseases. Epigeneticist and founder of Twins UK, Tim Spector was shocked when his research over the decades showed that identical twins, "didn't even *get* the same diseases, usually even if those diseases are very strongly genetic and very common like diabetes and heart disease" (Spector). Moreover, researchers at Johns Hopkins University found the same conclusions, explaining "the fact that both identical twins in a pair don't develop the disease 100% of the time indicates that other factors are involved" (NOVA). Research shows that "any

differences between twins are due to their environments, not
genetics…. Many environmentally induced differences are reflected in
the epigenome." A study looked at the epigenetics of identical twins
ranging in age from three years old to fifty years old, and found that
the epigenomes of the three-year-old twins were nearly identical while
the epigenomes of the fifty-year-old twins were almost entirely
different (NOVA). The young twins had not had time in life to
experience a range of different environments or behaviors, while the
other set of twins had had a half century to encounter a range of
different circumstances and habits. The years of differences are
reflected on their epigenetics. Examples like these seem to clearly show
differences from external factors: environments.

From these types of twin studies, we have learned that in some
cases our genetics can override our environments, and in some cases
our environments can override our genetics through epigenetics. Is it
possible then, to knowingly and purposefully alter our nature or
nurture? Rat studies show further evidence of environments altering
genetics. In one study, pregnant mother rats with a gene that caused
them to be fat and yellow, called the agouti gene, were feed specialized
food rich in vitamins like B-12, or folic acid, from which they could
make methyl tags which are responsible for creating epigenetic
silencing markers, that silence genes. The result was that the agouti
mother had several thin, brown babies due to the silencing markers on
their agouti genes (NOVA). Something as simple and age-old as a
proper diet, as part of our environment (or nurture) can have a
significant and lasting impact on us, and even our future generations.
In another rat study, two groups of mother rats were observed as either

very nurturing, by licking and cuddling their pups often, called "high-licking mothers," or more neglectful, spending much less time caring for their pups, called "low-licking mothers." Research found that both groups of rat pups were born with silencing markers around a gene that helps cope with stress, making the rats more prone to stress, but the pups of the high-licking mothers were found to have those same silencing markers missing a few weeks later. To test this, researchers switched the next set of litters and gave the pups of the high licking mothers to the low licking mothers to care for, and vice versa. The pups that were fostered by the high licking mothers also had the silencing markers missing from that gene a few weeks later, just like her own pups previously (NOVA). This is another remarkable example of how our nurture can have massive effects on our genetics and our future selves.

Science still has much to learn about the ways that nature and nurture interplay to make us who we are. However, it is clear that we are not stuck with one set destiny determined by nurture *or* nature alone. Cycles of fear can be overcome by knowledge since often learning more about snakes or even white rats can help us realize that they're not quite terrifying. Cycles of aggression may be overcome by positive environments and supportive influences since we often mimic the behaviors of those around us. Genetic predispositions do not mean genetic prophecy and can be overcome by healthy diets and lifestyles, since our epigenetics are affected by many aspects of our environments. In the many complexities that make us who we are, the common thread seems to be choice. Our choices affect our behaviors, perceptions and habits, which in turn affect our epigenetics and our identities. Although we cannot change the past, we can choose our present, and alter our futures.

In summary, we come with a fixed set of inherited genetics and personality predispositions at birth. However, beginning in childhood, and throughout life, our environments influence our behaviors and habits, as well as our epigenetics. In turn, our behaviors and habits can help alter the way that our genes behave and affect us throughout life. By exploring the nature vs. nurture debate, how they affect our identities, and seeing how we can alter our nature, nurture, and therefore our identities, too, it is evident that our nature and our nurture interplay to form our identities, and all remain malleable throughout our lifetimes. You are a genetic compilation of your parents, through DNA. I am a product of my raising, through environment. We all are a reflection of our experiences, through philosophies, behaviors and epigenetics. However, we are not just simply *one* of these, but rather *all of these,* things; they each combine, in one-of-a-kind ways, to make us uniquely who we are. Like multi-colored threads woven together to create a rich and intricately ornate tapestry, our genetics and environments are interwoven to form a rich and intricately ornate, multi-faceted, personality, one that can be altered through personal choice, if we so choose.

Works Cited

"Ghost in Your Genes" *NOVA*, PBS, Oct 16, 2007, Transcript,

    www.pbs.org/wgbh/nova/transcripts/3413_genes.html.

Healy, Melissa. "Personality Trait or Mental Disorder? The Same

    Genes May Weigh in on Both", *Los Angeles Times*, Dec 9, 2016,

    Web, www.latimes.com/science/sciencenow/la-sci-sn-personality-

    mental-illness-genes-20161208-story.html.

Singh, Maanvi. "Some Early Childhood Experiences Shape our Adult

    Lives, But Which Ones?", *NPR*, Dec 19, 2014, Web,

    www.npr.org/sections/health-

    shots/2014/12/19/371679655/some-early-childhood-experiences-

    shape-adult-life-but-which.

Spector, Tim. "Identically Different." *TEDx Talks King's College*, 23 May

    2013, London, YouTube,

    www.youtube.com/watch?v=1W5SeBYERNI.

Than, Ker. "A Brief History of Twin Studies", *Smithsonian*, March 4,

    2016. Web, www.smithsonianmag.com/science-nature/brief-

    history-twin-studies-180958281/.

Social Identity, The Sociocultural Way

Brady Marshall

Have you come to realize that not everyone's "social identity" is the same or even similar? When you see or hear the phrase "social identity," what do you think of? Do you picture an ID badge or someone holding one to represent who he/she is, or just a portrait of a person? Do you even think of a request of sensitive personal information about yourself, like your name, date of birth, address, phone number, and Social Security Number? Well, each person's social identity is actually a combination of a state of membership of the social categories and groups to which that person belongs, such as ethnic and religious groups and social roles, and the social norms of his/her lifestyle based on being a member of those groups and having the social roles they have. These personal properties are different for everyone, which is why not all people around the world appear similar or have the same set of rules to follow. It all explains how people from various ethnic and religious backgrounds live different lifestyles.

For starters, social identity, a theory introduced by Polish-born British social psychologist Henri Tajfel, is basically "a person's sense of who they are based on their group membership(s)" (McLeod, "Social Identity Theory"). Saul McLeod, the author of *Simply Psychology*, clearly explains the process of determining someone's social identity to see how each individual is socially different. The first step is to categorize other people and ourselves with well-understood social categories such as skin color, ethnicity, nationality, and religion, as well as social roles (McLeod, "Social Identity Theory"). Our social roles are the parts we play in our everyday lives, such as siblings, parents, friends, coworkers, customers, and authority figures. Professor McLeod admits that each and every social role gives us a set of rules of expected behavior to follow, called "norms." Our social norms are the rules of how each of us should behave in a social group that constitutes part of our identity (McLeod, "Social Roles"). For example, the way that authority figures, such as police officers, judges, members of the FBI, and the President, should act is not the same way that entertainers such as Hollywood actors and famous pop, rock, or country musicians should act, because these types of people have different social roles to play and thus have different social norms. Authority figures are supposed to act to help protect the general public and thus take socially and/or physically dangerous matters seriously, whereas musicians and actors are supposed to entertain people.

This explains how our membership in the social groups/categories to which we belong influences our social norms, according to social identification, the next step in discovering your social identity. Under McLeod's definition of social identification, "we adopt the identity of the group we have categorized ourselves as belonging to," which here means that we follow the norms of each social role we have (McLeod, "Social Identity Theory"). Professor McLeod provides an example of this: people who are categorized as students tend to develop the identity of a student by following the norms they think students have (McLeod, "Social Identity Theory"). Given that they really are students, that means they would attend classes on a regular schedule and listen to the teacher's lectures, study for forthcoming tests, and perhaps even read books and write to maintain intelligence, as well as apply what they're learning.

However, not everyone is subject to the same set of norms, because everyone has different social categories, which means not everyone's social identification is the same. The social norms of authority figures and famous entertainers are a good example of this. An authority figure, such as a police officer, and a famous entertainer, such as a Hollywood actor or a country or pop singer, are each socially identified differently, which means they each have different norms. In social comparison, the final step of determining people's social identity, a member of one social group or category differentiates a group to which he/she belongs from other groups by comparing the social properties of his/her own group to those of other groups, which helps us differentiate between the social identity of various people (McLeod, "Social Identity Theory"). A young man who works at an auto-parts store and a doctor are a perfect example of social comparison because they each have separate social norms at their job. The young man at the auto-parts store is supposed to satisfy customers by helping them find the products they are in search of for maintaining their vehicles, whereas the doctor is supposed to give check-ups to their clients and prescribe medicines to them as necessary.

Another clue about someone's social identity is his/her physical appearance. Each person appears physically different, which provides a clue about the ethnic group of which he/she is a member. For example, Europeans, Americans, or Australians with light-colored skin, especially white, are most likely Caucasian. But people with relatively light-colored skin whose eyes are relatively-oval, compared to those of Caucasians, are most likely Asian or Native American; and people whose skin is a relatively dark color, typically black or brown, are usually African, Latino, or Caribbean (Browne). Given these descriptions, ethnicity seems to be related to the race or skin color of a group of people, but they are really not the exact same thing. Ethnicity, as defined by Ken Browne, the author of the sociology textbook *Sociology for AS AQA*, is "the shared culture of a social group which gives its members a common identity in some ways different from other social groups" (Browne). So "ethnic identity" is "one [type of identity] where individuals assert their identity primarily in terms of the ethnic group and culture to which they belong, including values, beliefs, traditions, language, diet, dress and religious ideas. It is this [identity] that gives them meaning and a sense of belonging with others like themselves" (Browne 51-52). Individuals can have more than one social identity if their family's ancestors were members of different ethnic groups from different regions. Anyone who does has what Browne calls a "hybrid identity," the type of identity arising from membership of two or more social identities. An example of this that Browne provides applies to "British Asians," who may keep their ethnic Asian identity at home "through socialization from their family and ethnic group," but take on the cultural "white British" identity in public in the mainland Great Britain (Browne 57). For example, at home they might cook their foods by stir-frying them on a wok instead of a pan and never use an oven, as well as eat with chopsticks at every meal, which are traditional in the Chinese cuisine ("Desserts"). But British Asian students at school might use the silverware provided to them at the cafeteria at school.

In addition, members of one ethnic group who have emigrated from their native region may actually have at least two *ethnic* identities, because they inherit some cultural and genetic traits of their ethnic group's native region but also adopt some cultural traits of the main region where they live (Browne). For an example that Browne provides, African-Caribbean people inherit their black skin from their African ancestors and may be thankful for the dark color of their skin, wear dreadlocks, and like music such as hip hop and reggae the best, which are all cultural for Caribbean blacks (Browne 55).

Given that each ethnic group has different social norms, chances are people with a hybrid identity actually have to follow a combination of the social norms of their native ethnic group and the cultural norms of where they live. For example, African-Caribbean citizens of Great Britain may have a hybrid identity if they wear dreadlocks all the time and enjoy listening to hip hop and reggae music, which are cultural among Caribbean blacks, and go to the pub to socialize and enjoy alcoholic beverages and even visit the Queen, which are important in the British culture. And a Mexican-American family living in or around Springfield, Missouri, may celebrate Cinco de Mayo and Day of the

Dead, both of which are Mexican holidays, but also celebrate the Fourth of July and maybe even visit the Ozark Empire Fairgrounds, a local fair that happens every summer in Springfield.

Each person's religion is another aspect of his/her social identity and is often associated with his/her ethnicity and/or national residence, since people all over the world have different religious identities. *Actforlibraries.org* provides some examples of connections between religion and race/nationality: "People of European, African-American, and Latin American descent are typically Christian; people of Middle Eastern but not Israeli descent are typically Muslim; and people of eastern Asian descent are typically Buddhist" ("Religion is Social Identity").

Our religion typically has social norms, as our ethnicity does, which means that people of various religions tend to live different lifestyles. For example, Christian families are influenced by their religion to go to church on Sunday mornings and pray with other Christians ("Religion is Social Identity"). This applies to my family because we are Christian. I have gone to church with my mother every weekend when we could, and sometimes my mother and I tithe, which means to donate one-tenth of your income to your church. We also pray to God to thank Him for our blessings and on behalf of people and their difficulties, and I have prayed at meals and at bed every day for several months now. In addition, my mother listens to Christian music on the radio frequently. These are some of the main traditional norms that Christians have long had.

Both *Actforlibraries.org* and Ken Browne confess that our religion also limits our diet by forbidding us to eat particular foods ("Religion is

Social Identity;" Browne 56). For example, Hindus are prohibited to eat beef or drink alcohol and must fast for several days, and Muslims are prohibited to eat pork and some types of bird or drink alcohol or caffeine and must refrain from eating or drinking anything during certain eras (Browne 56; "Religion and Dietary Practices"). Buddhists, however, are forbidden to eat any meat and should take a vegetarian diet ("Religion and Dietary Practices").

Generally speaking, you can tell people's social identity by discovering their ethnicity and where their ancestors are from, their religion, and what their social roles are, as well as the social norms of their lifestyle. You can determine which ethnic group someone is a member of by studying that person's physical appearance. Factors such as the color of each person's skin and the shape of his/her eyes are clues about his/her ethnicity. You can also determine people's religion, as well as the nationality or ethnicity of their family, by their cultural and traditional behaviors and the holidays they celebrate and how they celebrate them. All of these factors make all people around the world socially different, so everyone's social identity is different. That means it is important for people from various backgrounds to understand one another's cultures to understand how one another is so different. So compare yourself to several other people with personal and social qualities different from your own. Consider their nationality, ethnicity, and religion, as well as the roles they play in their everyday lives. What do you think their social identity is as a whole? How would you describe your own social identity compared to theirs? How can you tell that your own social identity and theirs are what they are? Your own social identity is very probably different from that of many other people, since not everyone is in the same social categories, nor does everyone have the exact same group of norms, which is why people from various backgrounds all have different lifestyles to live.

Works Cited

Browne, Ken. "Culture and Identity." pp. 51–52, 55, 56, 57,

www.polity.co.uk/browne/downloads/BROWNE%20CHAPT

ER%202%20v2.pdf. Accessed 10 May 2017.

"Desserts." *Everyday Chinese*, Parragon Books Ltd, 2008, p. 218.

McLeod, Saul. "Social Identity Theory." *Simply Psychology*, 2008,

https://www.simplypsychology.org/social-identity-theory.html.

Accessed 1 Apr. 2017.

McLeod, Saul. "Social Roles and Social Norms." *Simply Psychology*, 2008,

https://www.simplypsychology.org/social-roles.html. Accessed

9 Apr. 2017.

"Religion and Dietary Practices." *Diet.com*, 12 Jan.

2017, www.diet.com/g/religion-and-dietary-practices. Accessed

10 May 2017.

"Religion is Social Identity." *Actforlibraries.org*, 7 Sept. 2016.

www.actforlibraries.org/religion-is-social-identity/. Accessed 1

Apr. 2017.

Not Who You Think I Am

Trystan Burris

"I hate millennials." If you have been following any major news outlet for the past several months, you will have heard this said at some point. This sentiment comes from many people saying that the younger generations are lazy and entitled. By this same token, the younger generations tend to think of the older generations as being "out of touch." These disconnects and differences are caused by our differing political and social values, as well as the environments in which each generation was raised. I have analyzed the three youngest generations and what has influenced them throughout their lives to explore and demonstrate how these factors can affect a person and a generation. As a millennial myself, I will also focus on the millennial experience throughout the rest of my research. This is due in part to the "fame" of the millennial generation in the sensationalist news media as well as my personal ties to the generation. I believe that a people's generation influences their identity by changing how they view themselves and others, by altering their political and social views, and by determining the environment of your upbringing.

A generation is a tricky thing to define. There are many ways that you could describe a person's generation, and these can include male-line and female-line generations. In general, however, a generation, as defined by Merriam-Webster, is "a body of living beings constituting a single step in the line of descent from an ancestor." This single step can be viewed from a very linear and simple point of view as the people that you went to K-12 school with. To get a better understanding of what defines a generation you must look at it in much broader terms. It is accepted as common knowledge that today, a generation will average around 25 years (Devine). This has been shorter, around 20 years, in the past. This is influenced by the age at which people have children and the average life expectancy of people.

Defining Generations

Just like your personal identity, generational identity is determined by a variety of outside factors. Each generation has a unique set of circumstances in which they are raised, and these circumstances change how they view the world and how they act in general. By examining individual generations, we can see these factors in action and understand how they influence us.

The baby boomers are one of the most well-known generations. People from this generation were born between the years 1946 and 1964. During this time, there was a lot of political upset stemming from various wars as well as the civil rights movement (Generational Differences). The Vietnam war was very influential on this generation, and it caused a lot of anti-war sentiment. This generation was behind events such as the landmark supreme court case Tinker v. Des Moines, when a group of students were removed from school for protesting the Vietnam War. As well, the parents of these children were survivors of the Great Depression, and this caused the "American dream" to be a very important factor for them growing up. This lead to the notion that they are greedy and self-centered. This generation was very idealistic however, advocating for human rights and protesting wars are defining events for them. They do not trust authority, and work hard to become better than their parents.

After the Baby Boomers came Generation X. Born between 1965 and 1980, this generation is very different from the boomers. Political unrest and distrust in the government was rampant during this period. Watergate and the tail end of Vietnam caused this generation to be wary and distrusting of their government, a big change from the previous generation that simply disagreed with it. The Cold War ended around this time, which means that this generation also grew up with the threat of nuclear war hanging over their heads. These kids also grew up around a time that the US was beginning to decline in international influence and power. The government is not the only thing that experienced large changes in this time. Technology saw huge advancements over this period. This generation grew up alongside modern technology, and thusly became accustomed to change and advancement with technology. The divorce rate also skyrocketed around this time, causing many children to become self-reliant and strong willed (Generational Differences). This increase in divorce rate seems to have changed how we view the American family, as we will see with the next generation. Self-reliant and adaptive, this generation distrusts their government and has a skeptical view of the world at large.

Finally, we have one of the most recent and most popular generations: The Millennials. Of any generation, this one gets the most media attention by far. Much of this is negative, as you can easily see from today's media cycle claiming that everyone "hates millennials." This generation is usually thought of as being born between 1981-2000, but those numbers can vary depending on who you talk to. This is the first generation in a long time to not be defined by war of some sort. Not to be without their fair share of violence though, this generation lived through one of the worst disasters in American history: the 9/11 terror attacks. The terror attacks did not just come from outside of the US though; school shootings became much more common over this period (Generational Differences). These attacks against innocents caused the parents of millennials to be very protective and shelter their children from "the evils of the world" (Generational Differences). Alongside terror attacks, divorce became very common by this point. This breakdown of the modern ideal family can be attributed, at least in part, to the generation before them and how they were raised. Also, this generation grew up with technology. This caused them to be very capable with technology, much more so than any generation before them. A group made up of realists, millennials seem to be concerned with the world on a global scale. This comes because of their early exposure to terror attacks and their sensitivity to them. As one of the most diverse generations, it fits that their defining moments are unique and different.

Labels

Despite all the different circumstances and events that seem to shape these generations, they are still just labels. They can never be one size fits all, and can never be all inclusive. There will always be people who break the mold, people who are different, and people who disagree with the ideals of their generation. Of the three generations listed above, millennials are the least likely to identify with their generational label (Most Millennials Resist the 'Millennial' Label). In fact, a study by the Pew Research Center shows that as time goes on, people are less likely to accept their generational labels. We see that around 79% of boomers identify as such, while GenX sits lower at 58%, and then we have millennials at low of 40% (Most Millennials Resist the 'Millennial' Label). While some of this can be attributed to age, one of the biggest causes for millennials to feel this way about their generation is the stereotypes given to them by today's media.

You can see it just about anywhere you look. From Buzzfeed and Breitbart to reputable news organizations such as the New York Times and the Washington Post, everyone loves to hate the millennial generation. Selfishness is central to all the accusations against millennials. Claims that "selfie culture" has created rampant narcissism are common (Stein). Entitlement goes along with selfishness as a common complaint levied against the generation. As to whether this is all true or not is up in the air and difficult to define because, as we have seen, many millennials do not identify with their generation at all. However, the effect that this message from the media can have on people is pronounced, and quite sad. The same Pew Research study found that 59% of millennials describe their own generation as self-absorbed while only 17% see their generation as having good morals (Most Millennials Resist the 'Millennial' Label). Over all, it seems that millennials are far less likely than any other generation before them to attribute positive labels to their own generation.

This onslaught from the media obviously influences the generation but it is important to imagine how this can affect an individual. As a member of this generation, you may begin to attribute these labels to yourself. As a millennial myself, I take great issue with the labels thrown around by the media and reject them. Over time though, this could wear on someone and begin to affect their individual identity as well as their sense of generational identity. While those two things are separate, generational identity can encompass almost all the environmental factors that make up your sense of self. From the way you were raised to the circumstances of your family, your generational identity is made of the same things that shape your personal identity.

A generation can be a very tricky thing to define, but it can also be tricky to classify because of the scenarios the generation was raised in. Those sets of circumstances set the foundation for a generation, and influence the general attitudes of the generation. Wars, government deception, and changing family values are all hugely impactful on a generation. Labels are also just as impactful. We see that labels given to millennials by the news media can cause many to attribute very negative things to their own generation. This causes many to reject their generational label all together. The circumstances of a person's upbringing and the labels given to that person by society, and himself, can change the way he/she thinks about themselves and others.

Works Cited

Devine, Donn. "How Long Is a Generation?" *Ancestry.com*.

    Ancestry.com. n.d. Web. 13 Apr. 2017.

    http://www.ancestry.com.au/learn/learningcenters/default.aspx?se

    ction=lib_Generation.

"Generational Differences Chart." *West Midland Family Center*.

    Wmfc.org. n.d. Web. 13 Apr. 2017.

    http://www.wmfc.org/uploads/GenerationalDifferencesChart.pdf

"Most Millennials Resist the 'Millennial' Label." *Pew Research Center*.

    People-press.org. 9 Sep. 2016. Web. 13 Apr. 2017.

    http://www.people-press.org/2015/09/03/most-millennials-resist-

    the-millennial-label/.

Stein, Joel. "Millennials: The Me Me Me Generation." *Time Inc*.

    Time.com. 20 May. 2013. Web. 13 Apr. 2017.

    http://time.com/247/millennials-the-me-me-me-generation/.

Age, Sex, Location

Hannah Winder

When a person is born, before he can even speak, he is given three labels. His parents and a team of nurses recognize his race, gender, and age with a single glance. This pattern continues as he grows. Others take a surveying look and can assume those three things, race, gender, and age, without a single word passing between. These assumptions have been made over and over for as long as humans have existed on the planet. It is a recently accepted idea, however, that these labels might change according to preference. Today, many individuals are identifying as a gender that is not their biological sex. Some others feel as though they belong to a different cultural or racial group than the group they were born into. There are even individuals who feel as though they are stuck in a certain age bracket or generation other than their own. What causes such radical internal change and what is the response when an individual decides to reflect this change outwardly?

It is often said that age is just a number. This is a nice sentiment to write in birthday cards but for some it holds much heavier meaning. It has been known, and often joked about, that some individuals may not identify with their chronological age. A 50 year old person may feel as though he is 35; or, in more rare and extreme cases, a 45 year old may feel as though he is a small child internally. How is this possible and why do people experience this displacement from their actual age? In their paper, John R. Logan, Russell Ward, and Glenna Spritze, claim that there are three major contributors to one's internal age (Logan, Ward, and Spritze 452). The first, and the most obvious, is one's chronological age. A person, though he may disassociate with his chronological age, is often aware of the number of years that he has lived. This can affect his perception of age and his own age identity. However, being aware of a number does not change internal age altogether. According to Gerben J. Westerhof, author of "Age identity" in the *Encyclopedia of the Life Course and Human Development*, a middle aged person is most likely to identify as thirteen years younger than their chronological age on average (Westerhof 11). A person who is aware of their actual age can feel as though they are a decade or more younger than they are in reality. This is not uncommon. Feeling as though one is stuck in a certain age in their life is even to be expected.

Health is the second contributor to internal age. It is no secret that declining health is associated with old age. Logan, Ward, and Spritze state in their article, "Older age and poorer health have been found to be consistent predictors of older age identities" (Logan, Ward, and Spritze 452). It follows logically that the better shape a person is in the younger he would feel. When a person is actively rebelling against his chronological age, he will often become more active and health conscious to keep up with the bodily ability he once had in his youth. This maintenance of physical ability is also seen by others and the individual is perceived as young therefore confirming his own perceptions of his age identity. However, there are signs of aging that cannot be stopped altogether. Signs like loss of eyesight and hearing, joint pain, gray hair, baldness, wrinkles, lack of energy, and loss of muscle mass present themselves as the years go by. These may be familiar because they are traditionally associated with age and the slow deterioration of the body. They can be slowed and covered up by hair dye or plastic surgery. All of this may help a person feel younger, but for someone who does not identify with their age they are not a permanent fix.

I interviewed Kori Little, a non-traditional student in one my college classes because we had previously discussed the topic of aging. I remember she mentioned that she did not feel her chronological age and in the interview she repeated the sentiment saying, "This is funny because I do not know how 51 supposed to feel... I would say I feel like I am in my 30's." This aligns with the research cited above. People in their mid life chronologically often do not identify with the number that is used to represent them. In the interview I decided to test a few theories I had learned about while doing research on this topic. The first was the topic of signposts. I asked Kori when she experienced major life changes and how mature they made her feel in comparison to her peers at the time. She told me that she had married at the age of 19 and since she was married at a young age she felt more mature than some of her friends but certainly not older. I then asked how her health and other factors affected her perception of age. She shared that she believes she has "the blessing of looking younger and internally feeling younger" and I have to say that after spending time with Kori, I agree. It is clear that she loves life and this gives her youth. It also seems that her surroundings affect her internal age as well. She mentioned that things like sunshine and being around younger students make her feel rejuvenated even if that was not always the case. As a non-traditional student, starting in school Kori was afraid of "acting like a mom all the time" but now she feels much less intimidated by her younger counterparts. Kori has chosen her age identity, an age that suits her more closely than any number could.

If age identity can be chosen, can everything about a person be his choice? If so, when can these choices go too far? The idea of racial identification is not new. There are many people who identify with their given cultural group. It is natural to feel at home with others who look, act, talk, and feel the way you do. This is why people, especially minorities, feel strong identification with their racial groups. However, when a person, born of one race, identifies with a culture separate from his birth race, questions and problems arise. This was the case of Rachel Dolezal, when the story of her race identity made headlines.

Rachel Dolezal was the president of the Washington chapter of the NAACP. She was an activist for racial equality and appeared to fit right into the African American culture. Looking at Rachel, it is evident that she is of African American decent with her tan skin, voluminous and very curly hair; even her fashion sense reflected her culture. She appeared to share the struggles of her fellow NAACP members and as a result was able to climb to high positions within the organization. It was not until June of 2015 that others discovered her birth race and she was forced to resign. It was evident to the media that Rachel had been putting on an elaborate show, making herself out to be a black woman.

Dolezal faced intense ridicule when the topic of cultural appropriation entered the conversation. Greg Bothelho, a reporter for

CNN quotes the NAACP President Cornell Brooks when he said, "just because one appreciates African American culture, doesn't mean you can disrespect the culture" (Bothelho). Many viewed Dolezal's charade as a display of white privilege; that she would claim to have the same struggles of a black person in a racially divided world. Some argues that Dolezal had spent most of her life physically white and enjoying the privileges of being white (Bothelho). If the struggles ever got too hard she had the option that biologically black people do not have; she could simply go back to her more Caucasian appearance and lifestyle.

Though the general opinion towards Dolezal was extremely negative, some defended her choice in identity. A popular comparison was to Caitlyn Jenner who had transitioned from male to female. Bothelho quotes a twitter user who posed an interesting question: "So Caitlyn Jenner is brave, but the internet wants to burn Rachel Dolezal at the stake. Are we bound to our bodies or not" (Bothelho)? It seems to be a double standard that biological sex and biological race are not given the same rules. It is becoming accepted that a transgender woman may have male genitals but identify as a woman. Why, then, is it unacceptable for a transracial African American to have been born with white skin but identify as black? Mirah Riben, of the Huffington Post, discusses this question by comparing Dolezal's situation to that of Asian adoptees. Riben reflects upon the views of some of these adoptees stating, "All felt White (on the inside) though they were not Caucasian, in much the same way Rachel Dolezal feels black" (Riben). Many of these teenaged Asian adoptees felt that they were physically Asian but otherwise identified with white culture. One of the teens, Haley, joked, "I'm a banana. I'm yellow on the outside and white on the inside" (Riben). Haley felt that her outward appearance did not reflect how she identified and how she wished to fit into social groups.

As for Dolezal using foundation and hair products to appear more physically black, she herself made a statement recorded by Bothelho: "I certainly don't stay out of the sun, I also don't put on blackface as a performance" (Bolthelho). It seems that this was not a game or a "performance" for Dolezal; it was her identity. This idea of body modification to make one's self appear to be more racially ambiguous is not new. Double eyelid surgery in Asian countries are wildly popular and in some cases expected. Many black women straighten their hair and still others use skin lighteners. These are all beauty modifications with the aim to appear more Caucasian. What is the difference, then, between these cosmetic choices and the choices of Rachel Dolezal if the black beauty standard is the standard she wishes to identify with? Dolezal quotes her son to CNN saying, "One of my sons yesterday (told me) 'mom racially you're human and culturally you're black'" (Bolthelho). It is important to remember that whatever a person identifies as internally, he is a human.

This lesson that one's physical appearance may not match his identity is especially relevant when discussing a hot topic of present politics, transgendered lifestyle. To be transgender is to identify apart from one's biological gender or sex. This, however can mean a number of things. Some people who identify as transgender feel that they fit in somewhere on a spectrum of masculine or feminine, and everywhere on the spectrum, preferences and ideas are vastly different. Others may feel gender-fluid, as though they do not identify strictly with either male or female but instead choose aspects of both genders. This is the case with Andrew Piotrowski, a transgender man who is still trying to sort out his gender fluidity.

I interviewed Andrew and gained insight into his mind and life. When I asked him if he had decided upon his gender identity, he said that for him it was hard to decide, and that because of this he would call himself gender-fluid. He went on to explain this by using his way of dress as an example. He said that he used clothing to express outwardly what he felt inwardly, as he gestured to his flat back hat and baggy shorts. However, he also told me that he still paints his fingernails because, though it is traditionally feminine, it is something he likes to do. He even remarked that one day he felt the urge to wear a dress and posted the whim on Facebook asking his friends, "Hey guys what would you think if I wore a dress today?" Andrew's post was met with mostly love and support, but the ideas of some transgendered people aren't as well received.

Many transgendered or transsexual people feel the need, and sometimes the pressure, to change themselves physically. This not only includes makeup, clothing, and wigs but procedures that can take months of healing and thousands of dollars. David Valentine, a trans man himself, recalls visiting a clinic with his friend Janet who was seriously considering a procedure. Valentine recalls that, "Janet could simply no longer sustain existence in a male body" (Valentine 203). This idea of being trapped is a sentiment shared by many transgendered people. Andrew tried to explain this feeling of wrongness to me by saying, "We aren't seeking attention. We were just born wrong. God didn't create us wrong. Being trans is not an act of God, it is an act of *ourselves*." This resonated with me because he emphasized that he chose his identity, that it slowly developed and became a realization. He identifies apart from his biological self because he chose to take that step to being closer to his true self, his most authentic identity.

Age, race, and gender are the most basic labels humans use to identify each other and themselves. When they change, the effects can be unusual, uncomfortable, and met with controversy. Despite all these obstacles, though, is it not worth it to find an identity that more closely reflects what is true inside? The idea of youth, the outward appearance of race, the dissonance between biological sex and idealized gender, all of these things make up parts of identity. These parts of identity cannot be ignored if a person wishes to live a fulfilling life. Through the stories of Kori, Rachel, and Andrew it is plain to see that at the core each person is a human, striving to match his thoughts and perceptions to his sense of self. Every day these struggles persist and internal battles rage on. This is why it is so crucial to remember that the labels a person is born with can only dictate his life if he allows them to.

Works Cited

Botelho, Greg. "Rachel Dolezal, Ex-NAACP Leader: 'I Identify as Black'." *CNN*. Cable News Network, 17 June 2015. Web. 13 Apr. 2017.

Logan, John R., Russell Ward, and Glenna Spitze. "As Old as You Feel: Age Identity in Middle and Later Life." *Social Forces* 71.2 (1992): 451. JSTOR [JSTOR]. Web. 12 Apr. 2017.

Mascarelli, Amanda Leigh. "Identifying as a Different Gender." *Science News for Students*. Society for Science and the Public, 21 Mar. 2017. Web. 13 Apr. 2017

Riben, Mirah. "Being Blackish: Race and Self-Identification." *The Huffington Post.com*. TheHuffingtonPost, 22 June 2015. Web. 13 Apr. 2017.

Valentine, David. "Sue E. Generous: Toward a Theory of Non-Transexuality." *Feminist Studies* 38.1 (2012): 201-08. JSTOR. Web. 20 Apr. 2017.

Westerhof, Gerben J. "Encyclopedia of the Life Course and Human Development". Ed. Deborah S. Carr. Detroit: Macmillan Reference USA, 2009. Print.

Lost and Found

Jana Kim

Who am I? It's a question that always tends to float around in my head. As an Asian-American woman, this topic was and still is something that I struggle with because I often get confused as to who I am and where I belong. Growing up in a predominately white community was confusing because my race was so different from those who surrounded me. There are so many factors that mash together to create a personality and identity. I strongly believe that my race, who I'm expected to be, and my environment affect my true self—both negatively and positively. With these three aspects, I eventually formed a persona for myself to show the world; in other words, I was being shaped into who I am today by understanding who, what, and where my influences were coming from.

There are many people who confuse ethnicity and nationality, but there is a big difference between them. Ethnicity is a certain group a person identifies himself or herself as racially, religiously, or culturally. On the other hand, nationality is the political state a person belongs to. I am ethnically Korean because of my race and culture, but my nationality is American because I am a U.S. citizen. Growing up, this whole idea of belonging to two different groups distracted me from being who I wanted to be. I was born and raised in America, but I'm not Caucasian. Still to this day, people have a difficult time wrapping their heads around the fact that I can be Asian and be born in America at the same time. For the longest time, I denied my culture—my native language, food, lifestyle, etc.—because I was afraid of being different from everyone around me. When middle school started, everything I did became "too Asian"— as my classmates would say. During lunch, we had the option to eat chicken and rice and although I wanted to eat it, I would never go close to it because I got teased for wanting something that was considered Asian. Then, I began to reject my native tongue. When my family and I were out in public, I told them not to speak Korean because people would start looking—which didn't please my parents very much. Following that incident, when people asked me if I spoke Korean, I quickly denied it even though I was and still am very fluent. This went on for years and in the midst of it all, I forgot my identity. I attempted to conform to the lifestyle and personality traits of my Caucasian friends and for a while, I despised being around people who were Asian. Everyone I was surrounded by thought I was overreacting, but they weren't a race other than Caucasian—they weren't used to the daily remarks that reminded them that they were different. I put the pressure of conforming on myself and it became chaotic because I was trying to please both my Caucasian and Asian parts of my life.

There are many stereotypes that surround the Asian ethnicity. Out of the many descriptions, the ones that affected me the most were that all Asian people are smart, they all have strict families, and they're not good at English. These three stereotypes might seem generic or it may seem like I'm overreacting, but those small comments eventually got into my head. I didn't want to be smart. I became so self-conscious that I started to fail my assignments on purpose. I became someone who didn't like trying hard and everything I did was second-rate. I actually disliked being called intelligent because people would always attach the words, "…because she's Asian." I wanted to be smart because I studied hard, not because I was an ethnicity that had a stereotype of being brilliant. In fact, my parents never made me study, which brings me to the second point: all Asian families are strict. In high school, my friends would always ask, "Are your parents okay with you staying out past 7? Aren't your parents going to make you study?" or "Wow, I never knew Asian parents would allow you to watch this movie with us." These remarks made me want to do the opposite of what they were saying and my personality was yet again changed and altered into something that I'm still trying to fix today. After graduating high school, my environment changed drastically. I never saw any of the people I was used to seeing every day in school and I began going to a Korean-American church. At this point, I was still confused because I had different personalities when I was around different ethnic groups. My environment had a huge role in developing my personality because both races act and react to situations differently. For example, when I was around Korean people, my manners, speaking tone, and body language became more modest and feminine; however, around my Caucasian friends, I became more energetic and sarcastic in my speech. At a certain point, I was tired of switching around and I realized I needed to balance out both sides. Attending a

Korean-American church actually helped me in the process of accepting who I was. My friend group slowly started to become the youth group at the church (which was made up of mostly Asian people) and I started to become comfortable with who I was inside. Accepting the Korean part of me was the first step in coming out of my shell to find a middle ground between the two ethnicities. I chose to surround myself with friends from both ends who would accept both parts of me and I believe that is what helped me to create an identity that shows my true self.

According to The Encyclopedia Britannica, the persona is, "…the personality that an individual projects to others, as differentiated from the authentic self" (Encyclopedia Britannica). It's a term that Carl Jung came up with and he explains that it's a role that is played by a person depending on the environment he or she is surrounded by. In a psychological point of view, I created a persona that I interchanged when I was with different groups of people. The Encyclopedia also states that, "…the persona enables the individual to adapt to society's demands." In order to feel like I belonged in both crowds, I created two masks that I took on and off to fit in with these polar opposite groups of people. When I became more familiarized and comfortable with my Asian side, my persona and my authentic self met and created a middle ground.

Although the journey was long, my race, my environment, and who I was expected to be gave me experiences that shaped my identity. I strongly believe that who I surround myself with has a large part in my personality because it can change how I act in an instant. When my persona and my inner self became one, I became my true self by taking parts of me from each side and creating a harmony between them.

Works Cited

"Persona", Encyclopedia Britannica, Encyclopedia Britannica, inc., 12 May 2005. Accessed 19 Apr. 2017.

Fighting Gender Conformity in Religious Institutions: Behind the Scenes of Baptist Life for Women and Eliminating the Stigma of the 'F' Word

Cally Chisholm

If God decided Mary and Joseph were to deliver a baby with two X chromosomes, would Christianity exist? In other words, would there be a Christian church if Jesus had been a woman? To ponder that question, it's important to face the reality of sexism in our world. It's no secret that women have always been treated like second-class citizens, today and even more so in biblical times. For centuries, women have been fighting tirelessly to be treated as equals in the church, and gender equality is critical to the future relevance of the Baptist church for the 21st century woman who may not be willing to embrace traditional gender roles. As such a woman, I have faced many subtle indications that I am not to cross certain boundaries. Although shouldering the weight of others' expectations, I was fortunate to grow up with a pastor as my father. I've seen and heard the "behind the scenes" of how a Baptist church functions, which gives me a unique perspective to the gender role issue. But, while societal pressure remains, I can look to the influence of prominent women in the Bible whose actions and contributions have been greatly diminished over time. There are numerous examples of Jesus praising women for their boldness and welcoming them into his circle despite the intense sexism of their patriarchal society; I'm curious why Christian churches aren't following this particular example of Jesus, too. It's difficult to reconcile that Christian congregations passionately believe that Jesus rose from the dead, while remaining "on the fence" about this issue. Thankfully, my current church family proudly affirms women in ministry, so it has become easy for me to take that for granted. I have had the opportunity to see women leading worship and even preaching from the pulpit. Unfortunately, many other women are influenced by churches who limit their leadership roles–they adapt to the gender box and learn to merely survive in it. Fortunately, I am breaking free of that stereotype without sacrificing my faith, so I can live the way I choose. I identify as a Christian woman and a feminist, and I have decided that they are not mutually exclusive.

To understand the root of sexism in Baptist life and religious institutions in general, it's important to know the key terms that explain the attitude towards women and gender roles. Most of the gender roles in society have had more influence on today's Baptist churches than would like to be admitted. The church is known for its antiquated beliefs that describe how people should live solely based on gender. Another word for this is **creedalism**. Merriam Webster Dictionary describes this term as an "undue insistence upon traditional statements of belief" ("Creedalism"). Because those who push for this idea believe they have a concrete understanding of how the world works, men and women alike are used to having and being surrounded by similar family units. This example of conformity is applied by actively enforcing patriarchal interpretations of scripture based on how the society functions at the time. **Conformity**, as defined in Merriam Webster Dictionary, is an "action in accordance with some specified standard or authority or to social custom" ("Conformity"). Ever since the beginning of human creation, women have been perceived to be an extended part of their husbands, which means that females have only recently in history have been able to live as their own persons. It is similar to how the dog is proudly affirmed as "man's best friend". Women have been treated and viewed as man's best possession. Because of this, women who are persuaded by creedalism-based church environments are usually unaware of life paths separate from men, marriage, and children. Typically, requirements for many women like this include being a devoted wife and bearer of children. They are the stay-at-home moms that cook the meals and fold the laundry for a living. This idea of a woman's role in society is not necessarily a bad one per se, because many women may claim to want this role. However, many women believe that this is the only path to happiness and fulfillment, because of how their church and family interpret the Bible's statements about their identity.

Another reason women are limited is because some people have used scripture from the Bible to justify sexism. Another key term to know is an **inerrancy**. In the book *Putting Women in Their Place* by Audra and Joe Trull, this term is explored through many different definitions. More specifically, *naive inerrancy* describes the process of the Word as written by God with little or no involvement of human persuasion (Trull). Having this perception of God can be troubling to feminist women like myself, because there are many verses that discourage female participation. For example, in 1 Corinthians 14:34-35, the Apostle Paul called for women to be dependent on men: "Let women remain silent in the churches, for it is not permitted for them to speak; rather let them remain submitted, just as the Law also says. And if they want to learn anything, let them ask their own husbands at home, for it is a shameful matter for a woman to speak in church" (1 Corinthians 14:34-35). So, as a nontraditional Christian woman, I have to approach these particular kinds of verses with a grain of salt and **hermeneutics.** This is described as "the study of the methodological principles of interpretation" ("Hermeneutics"). Theologian Elizabeth Johnson, who wrote the book *She Who Is*, describes her pre-screening of scripture by keeping in mind that "the texts as such were written mostly by men and for men in a patriarchal cultural context" (Johnson 76). This is absolutely true of the Bible. But, fortunately for us, one of the world's most recognized figures in history was sent to not only die for our sins, but to shake up the social hierarchy.

Jesus Christ had many female followers; he didn't ignore them or "put them in their place." Many of them were witnesses to miracles and were actively involved in his journey on Earth. For example, in the

Gospel of John 12:1-8, Mary (not his mother; there are many different women named Mary in the scriptures. Some scholars believe that this is Mary Magdalene, but it is not for certain) felt so liberated by Jesus that she committed what was then a taboo act–she let down her hair and anointed his feet with perfume, and despite protests from Judas Iscariot (who was one of Jesus' followers and betrayer), Jesus affirmed Mary's actions. Also, Magdalene, along with Joanna, and Mary, the mother of James, were the first witnesses to His resurrection (The Bible, Luke 24). Magdalene was also the first to speak to Jesus after his crucifixion and resurrection (The Bible, John 20:14-18). Ironically, according to the well-known Jewish historian and author, Flavius Josephus, women in first century Rome could not testify legally in courts (Josephus 4:219). Even after she and the other women attempted to share the Good News, the 12 male disciples thought they were speaking nonsense. This revolutionary event is not merely the pinnacle of the Christian faith, but women were the first messengers. Jesus' connection to his female followers is the most underrated aspect of Jesus' time on Earth. Women are usually mentioned in passing.

Because these opinions are so dear to me, I have difficulty connecting to other Christian women my age. I grew up in church. My dad is a pastor and my mother is active in the church by teaching college students, singing in the choir, and working for a Christian female author and speaker these past few years. I have dealt with all sorts of judgments growing up, and because of who my parents are, I heard all sorts of comments about my appearance. I lost count of the number of times I've been told: "You're getting so big, pretty soon you'll be getting married and having children." This doesn't necessarily offend me, but it is quite troubling to hear when you're 16-17 years old and still in high school trying to figure out your purpose in life. Usually, it would make sense for a pastor's daughter who grew up in Mississippi, Tennessee, and spent the majority of her life in Missouri to feel indifferent about this issue, but it obviously has had the opposite effect on me. My parents always taught me the value of education and hard work. They supported me when I got my first job even though it took a lot of time away from home, and shared in my excitement for school projects and good grades. Many young women have a difficult time discovering who they are, but when involved in a socially conservative church setting, that can make it even more difficult. I still have trouble defining myself—I wouldn't describe myself as the traditional Christian woman. Sure, I enjoy wearing makeup when I choose to and can appreciate a good church outfit, but those things don't embody who I am on the inside. That shouldn't determine my intelligence or social status. I don't have to conform to what the majority of my religion thinks or believes about how I should live my life purely based on generalizations. I can still think for myself and hold on to my relationship with Jesus with no sacrifice or compromise. God's kingdom and Earth *do not* follow the same rules. It's time for more Baptist churches to realize that.

A predominant group of Christian churches are members of the Southern Baptist Convention (SBC). Members of this group openly believe that the role of pastor is limited to men, among other specificities relating to gender roles. According to an article by Jonathan Siktberg in Christian Ethics Today, this convention thrived for decades; differences used to be tolerated at one point. But in 1979, two fundamentalists (they believe that the Bible is inerrant, literal, and reject women in any leadership role) by the names of Paul Pressler and Paige Patterson, took over the SBC (Siktberg 7). It soon became clear that they took over the SBC to promote their own agenda onto churches. It wasn't until 1998 that the SBC released their "Baptist Faith and Message" report that stated "a wife is to submit graciously" to her husband without expecting the same in return (Siktberg 8). Then, in 2000, the fundamentalist view became a much more prominent spectacle that "destroyed those freedoms that have united Baptists across centuries: religious freedom, individual freedom, freedom to interpret the Bible, and freedom of the local church" (Siktberg 9). Also, drastic steps were taken to ensure the fundamentalist view was being taught and embraced. They took over all six SBC seminaries (higher education for aspiring Christian leaders) by forcing faculty to sign their "Baptist Faith and Message" document that included the statement regarding women. Those who refused to conform to this incredibly sexist and restrictive outline of SBC beliefs, took a stand and many lost their jobs as a result (Siktberg 9). After the split of the SBC, a new community of faith was born called the Cooperative Baptist Fellowship (CBF) that affirms women in ministry. I am proud to say that I belong to a church that upholds the CBF's statement about women and affirms female leaders.

My father currently serves as Senior Pastor for University Heights Baptist Church which is the only Baptist church in the Ozarks that affirms women in pastoral ministry. This is a troubling reality check for how far we still have to go. My church is considered to be **egalitarian**. Churches like mine practice the "belief in human equality especially

with respect to social, political, and economic affairs"
("Egalitarianism"). In addition to being a member and intern for my
inclusive church, I've been fortunate to see many different women
stand at the pulpit to preach. For example, every few years we have
Rev. Muriel Johnson, Associate Minister of American Baptist Churches
preach, and just recently welcomed Molly Marshall, President and
Professor of Theology and Spiritual Formation at Central Baptist
Theological Seminary, to give a sermon. We also have several female
deacons as well who serve and work an important role in the church. It
is important for young girls and women to see themselves in the people
that lead worship, so that they can recognize their own potential. Even
if they don't see themselves as a pastor, they can still feel more
confident about themselves.

While Baptist churches are more complicated and diverse in their
views of women than most people realize, a lot of churches still have
trouble embracing the feminist movement because of the progressive
and liberal politics that come with it. While politics plays a role, the
feminist definition is a pretty simple one to embrace: "the theory of the
political, economic, and social equality of the sexes" ("Feminism").
Pam Durso is the executive director of Baptist Women in Ministry,
which supports all women in Baptist life, and she is a "loud and proud"
feminist. In an email interview with me, she said, "...women should
have equal access to leadership roles and should receive equal pay. But
my stance is based more on my theological understanding that God
created females and males in God's image, and thus, God's design was
for there to be equality between the genders" (Durso). It is important
for young girls and women to understand that there is nothing wrong

with identifying as Christian and feminist. Also, it's important to eliminate the stigma of associating the movement as "anti-man." That is simply not the case. Feminism is not a dirty word and does not diminish your credibility as a Christian.

I have formed a wild theory that Jesus Christ was the kickstarter of the entire feminist movement. One of the events that supports my theory is recorded in the Gospel of John 8:1-11; He literally saved an unnamed woman's life after a mob of Pharisees (religious male leaders) brought her to him after she was caught in an act of adultery. They wanted Jesus to condemn her to a painful and deadly stoning as punishment. Instead of playing into the hands of his skeptics, Jesus gave them a challenge: "Let the one who has never sinned throw the first stone" (The Bible, John 8:1-11). The mob was dumbfounded by his response, and Jesus stayed with the woman until everyone had left and gave her the same advice he gives everyone: "Go and sin no more" (The Bible, John 8:11). Jesus' inclusion and affirmation of women recognized that both sexes are equal in the eyes of God. The reason why so many women find comfort in Christianity despite the sexism is that Jesus effortlessly treated everyone the same without holding females to a different standard.

My gender plays a part in how I perceive theology. As a woman, I notice when women are ignored and weighed down by old interpretations of the Bible. Christ's feminist actions seems to have been overlooked by strict Baptist churches who are stuck in the past and refuse to open their minds to the 'F' word. The only reason why some Baptists, both men and women alike, have a difficult time accepting female leaders and ministers is because it has not become normalized. Although progress has been made, there is still a lot of ground to cover. It is a challenge for young girls who are struggling to figure out who they are when they have sexist influences constantly chipping away at their confidence and dignity. Church should be a place where anything with God is possible, and sadly that belief is not being upheld by those who claim to understand it. These sexist beliefs and intolerance are not helping to bring millennials into the Christian faith. In our email interview, Durso commented on how to attract young women to church: "I believe and I also practice, we must invite young women into leadership roles, invite them to use their gifts, invite them to use their voices. We have to make room for them as leaders *now* and not just tell them that they are future leaders" (Durso). Real change won't happen if churches continue to put off this issue, and in the process are neglecting to care for their congregation.

Conformity in Baptist churches is a major issue caused by creedalism. While the treatment of women has remained unchanged, Jesus Christ displayed feminist beliefs by accepting and affirming his female followers. Despite this, there are many Baptist churches who believe differently about gender roles, but having the chance to experience women leaders in worship has helped me understand my own potential. Gender and religion play significant roles in shaping many people's lives and have the capacity to either have positive or negative influence on future generations. Personally, my faith has had a positive influence on my life, and I owe that to my parents and church family who have helped me grow into a strong, independent woman. While I don't see myself filling my father's shoes career-wise, I know that I can make great change in the world with the talents I've been given by God.

Works Cited

"Creedalism." *Merriam-Webster*. Merriam-Webster, n.d. Web. 11 Apr.
    2017.

"Conformity." *Merriam-Webster*. Merriam-Webster, n.d. Web. 11 Apr.
    2017.

Durso, Pam. E-mail interview. 10 Apr. 2017.

"Egalitarianism." *Merriam-Webster*. Merriam-Webster, n.d. Web. 11 Apr.
    2017.

"Feminism." *Merriam-Webster*. Merriam-Webster, n.d. Web. 11 Apr.
    2017.

"Hermeneutic." *Merriam-Webster*. Merriam-Webster, n.d. Web. 11 Apr.
    2017.

Johnson, Elizabeth A. *She who is: the mystery of God in feminist theological
    discourse*. New York: Crossroad, 2002. Print.

Josephus, Flavius. "The Antiquities of the Jews, 4.219." *Flavius Josephus,
    Antiquities of the Jews 4.219*. Lexundria, n.d. Web. 11 Apr. 2017.

Siktberg, Jonathan. "A Story Every Baptist Should Know: a
    Convention Lost and a Fellowship Born." *Christian Ethics Today*.
    Christian Ethics Today Foundation, n.d. Web. 11 Apr. 2017.

Trull, Joe E., and Audra E. Trull. *Putting women in their place: moving beyond
    genderstereotypes in church and home*. Macon, GA: Smyth & Helwys
    Pub., 2003. Print.

Soul Murder: Psychological Identity Theft

J. Abigail Cool

I was only 17 when I fell in love with a boy that captured my heart. I was spunky, bubbly, outgoing and active in my high school classes, sports, and church activities. At first things in our relationship seemed wonderful, but slowly odd things began to happen. He started asking for a level of loyalty from me that didn't seem right. He pressured me to leave my friends behind. He became jealous of any time that I didn't spend with him. He even convinced me to throw my guitar in a water well to prove my devotions were only to him. Deep inside, there was a part of me that felt that something was wrong, but somehow, between late night calls, love letters, and a proposal for marriage, I pushed those feelings down. The night before our wedding, while sitting in his car, those feelings and fears reemerged and so I announced that the wedding was to be called off. I left the vehicle but he forced me back into the car and somehow convinced me to marry him. From that time forward, through all the battering, isolation, accusations, and public humiliation, while raising five children, I somehow, narrowly escaped the situation with just a thread of my identity, the only part left that he didn't steal.

We all know about the destructive crime of identity theft that is the fraudulent acquisition and use of a person's private identifying information, usually for financial gain. Yet there's another kind of identity theft that deserves our attention. You might date and marry someone who could steal the very core of your being and not know in the end how it happened. And, not being informed can thereby greatly impact not only your identity and well-being but your future, your future children, and their futures. Meeting a partner is a normal and wonderful experience, but there are signs to be mindful of that indicate the relationship is not a healthy one. When an individual is subjected to the controlling power of another person, you might not detect it at first. The steps are subtle, systematic and even calculated actions that can steal the essence of your being. It is this psychological identity theft that needs to be better understood by friends, family, churches and community. If we stand by and ignore the signs, the need for help will go undetected. In failing to help, we bear some responsibility for the final wreckage of an individual or a family. We can, by default, betray an abused individual and increase their powerlessness. Ignorance can be costly to not only the emotional constitution of individuals, but the cost for our communities' services, hospitals and other agencies is in the billions. While these are all terrible tolls, the greatest and most destructive cost is the perpetual cycle of abuse that affects generations of families. Though there are many ways to psychologically steal identity. I will present but a few ways of how this can happen to anyone. I hope to be able to raise awareness by presenting some of my own experiences beginning at age 17 and spanning 36 years, along with the research of trauma professionals, the medical field and battering intervention specialists to describe some of the patterns with which a partner can systematically overpower, interpret, steal, and even murder a person's identity.

A term that is often used to describe the initial stages that a partner uses to accomplish psychological identity theft is "grooming." Grooming is the tactic of overcoming the survivor's defenses. Grooming works by mixing positive behaviors with elements of abuse. Detecting any sort of mistreatment early in the relationship is difficult. Michael Samsel, DSHS Certified Domestic Violence Perpetrator Treatment Provider and author of the website, *Abuse and Relationships*, reveals how covert the process is and how the victim experiences mixed emotions and intermittent confusion: "Because the primary aggressor's real goal isn't understood by the [victim], she often misses the harmful implications and dismisses the internal signals of alarm that do arise" (Samsel). Samsel continues to point out that "[a]t the beginning, all behaviors are positive. Slowly, abusive elements are added in amounts that surprise the survivor to an extent, but do not push alarm to a high level. Over time, the inappropriate comes to feel normal."

Judith Herman, M.D., author of the groundbreaking book, *Trauma and Recovery, the Aftermath of Violence. From Political Terror to Domestic Violence* explains how a victim over time ultimately surrenders her will to the power of a controlling partner. The final effects of such control can result in chronic post-traumatic stress disorder. Herman reveals that the steps start early in the relationship as in this experience of a woman who imperceptibly began to surrender parts of herself while being in love but conflicted by his unusual requests: "He didn't hit me, but he got very angry . . . He asked me a lot of questions about who I had been out with before I knew him and he made me bring from the house a whole file of letters and photographs and he stood over me as I stood over an open drain in the road and I had to put them in one by one— tear them up and put them in" (Herman).

Personally, I have never met this woman, but our experiences are identical. While dating my boyfriend, I often played the guitar for my friends around the campfire. As my relationship developed, I soon learned that any friendship or past relationship was to be abandoned to prove utter devotion to him only. He pressured me to throw my guitar into a water well in a ritualistic manner. Dropping the guitar into the well was the genesis of stealing the essence of who I was, but the deed was cloaked in devotion and appearances of deep love. Again, Herman's insight on this, pointing out that "[t]he destruction of attachments requires not only the isolation of the victim from others but also the destruction of her internal images of connection to others. For this reason, the perpetrator often goes to great lengths to deprive his victim of any objects of symbolic importance" (Herman). This explanation and my experiences support the idea that grooming is subtle and imperceptible in the process of psychological identity theft. Though very difficult, if we can learn to recognize these things sooner, we may be able to avoid moving into the next level of the loss of identity.

Once a partner/perpetrator has successfully lured in his victim, he can then achieve deeper levels of entrenchment through such things as isolation. You don't recognize the isolation at the first but it does increase over time. His words convey and convince you that parents and friends or instructors don't have your best interest in mind, that he is the only one that loves you. You begin to shove down your own reasoning. The front door is open and the keys are on the table, but it's as if you're being held captive by a silken thread and by the time you are fully aware, resistance is futile. Herman draws distinct parallels the way a political terrorist isolates his captives, and the way a partner isolates his victim. According to Herman, "The emotional bond that develops between a battered woman and her abuser, though comparable to that of a hostage and captor, has some unique aspects based on the special attachment between victim and perpetrator in domestic abuse" (Herman).

Beginning early February 1974, Patricia Hearst, a nineteen year old student living in Berkeley, California was abducted by a left-wing terrorist group known as the Simbeonese Liberation Army and was held hostage for 19 months. Her captors, through the psychological methods of isolation and control, managed to break her self-will down to the point that she joined them in their terrorist activities. Doing so was the only way to survive. She was kept starving, in a closet, confined in filthy conditions. She was manipulated to agree with her captors. She said, "They allowed me to eat with them at times and occasionally I sat blindfolded with them late into the night . . . listening to their discussions. I was bombarded with [their] interpretations on life, politics, economics, social conditions, and current events. To maintain my sanity their reality became my reality" (Herman). The captors used episodes in which she was favored and then treated inhumanely by filthy isolation and demoralizing threats.

Michelle Maiese, author of the article "Dehumanization," writes for *Beyond Intractability*. This organization publishes information about conflict resolution nationally, internationally, and with individuals and their communities. But there are times when restoring relationships is not possible due to what she defines as "dehumanization." It is a mindset of an aggressor who views an individual as non-human, separate, unequal or brands their subject with less than human labels and treatment. In doing so, it is easier for the aggressor to take control over and abuse another human being. Consequently, they distance themselves from the atrocity of what they are doing. Maiese explains it this way, "Dehumanization is the psychological process of demonizing the enemy, making them seem less than human and hence not worthy of humane treatment. This can lead to violence, human rights violations, war crimes and genocide" (Maiese).

Hearst's demise was that her captors had so completely overpowered her will and identity that she eventually became an integral part of the terrorist group and even led the march with a machine gun to rob a San Francisco bank. In my personal experience, I too had become a captive through the power of being isolated. In attempts to please my husband, I complied with the bombardments of his words, whether I agreed with them or not. Any suggestion of a reality that was different from his was met with berating and accusations of being mentally ill, adulterous or being forced to comply by physical restraint. To resist was considered rebellion against not only him, but God. Our own children were included in the barrage at their early stages of development. I was forced to surrender to his interpretations of me, or lose what was most dear to me, my family. Herman describes the phenomenon, pointing out that when "a person is completely powerless, and any form of resistance is futile, she may go into a state of surrender. The system of self-defense shuts down entirely. The helpless person escapes from her situation not by action in the real world but rather by altering her state of consciousness" (Herman). As in the final demise of Patricia Hearst, so it was with my experience. Without the availability of any other input from any other human being, I finally surrendered and altered my own consciousness to comply with the demands of my husband. I composed a written "repentance" in which I debased myself in agreement with his interpretations of my being, my very identity. This writing was printed and distributed to over 300 people at church. Another portion of my identity was stolen in the fight for survival. Both Hearst and I were so imposed upon through severe and long term methods that vacillated between favor and threatening behavior that we acted out in ways that were not true to ourselves. This shows that the theft of someone's psychological identity has dire consequences through a series of methodical patterns and stages, usually in an environment of isolation.

Another powerful method employed by partners to alter and eventually destroy the victim's identity is by using other people. He will convince them of his interpretations about the victim to gain additional control. He will use their misled understandings of the situation and brow beat the victim with what they allegedly said about you. This alone increases the isolation of the victim and ensures that no one will offer personal support. And, this method ensures that he won't be exposed. Most human beings regard children with protective tenderness and respect. An aggressor who has already dehumanized you will not see your own children any differently. He views them as pawns to justify himself and uses them to support what he is doing. Though he feigns great love for the children, he is merely using them for his own benefit. This is purely an act of power and dominance. My own daughter wrote the following while she was in her late teens, describing what she experienced with her own father at only nine years old: "Not only did he use me to spy on my mother, he used me as his confidant regarding his finances, spiritual/religious issues, his employment/business, his children, and all about his issues with my Mother and with sex. He would comfort me and my siblings after he had beaten down my mother and led me to believe that my mother was mentally ill" (Cool). For my daughter to try to stand up to her father at such a young age was not possible. As he used the children, he was grooming them for further exploitation

Even more heartbreaking than watching a father use his children against their mother is realizing how the father is affecting his children personally. For example, when a young boy witnesses his mother being abused, he has two choices in the event of traumatic terror. He can either identify with the father or adopt the idea that abuse of a woman is acceptable, or he can feel the rage for how wrong the abuse is, which generally leads to guilt and shame for not being strong enough to stop the abuse. Either way, a choice is forced upon him and his own identity is compromised. Female children are deeply affected as well. They learn to accept that being abused is normal and often grow up to find mates that will continue the same pattern of abuse. The children, particularly girls who have been victims of sexual molestation, will likely develop depression, and low self-esteem. According to the Adverse Childhood Experiences research studies conducted by Kaiser Permanente and funded by the United States Justice Department, "children who witness these kinds of violence are at risk for potential substance abuse issues which can result in a diminished life span by twenty years" (Kaiser-Permanente). Dr. Shengold, clinical professor of psychiatry at the New York University of Medicine, has formulated a modern psychiatric term, "soul-murder." He says, "Soul murder is neither a diagnosis nor a condition . . . it is a crime" (Shengold). He explains how an abuser eradicates or compromises the separate identity of another person. He also mentions invading children mentally and sexually, specifically saying, "children are the usual victims of soul murder because their complete physical and emotional dependence on adults renders possible the tyranny of the child" (Shengold). The very act of violence imposes an identity upon the child not of his own volition. Lundy Bancroft, batterer intervention specialist and author of *Why Does He do that? Inside the Minds of Angry and Controlling Men,* explains what happens to children witnessing abuse or are being abused: "In the children's eyes, the abuser is simultaneously hated and revered. They resent his bullying and selfishness but are attracted to his charm and power. They soak up the delicious moments when he is kind and attentive. They may have an active fantasy life about getting big enough to stand up to him" (Bancroft). They rarely ever do. They've seen what he is capable of and on the other hand, sadly, "may hope to win their father's approval by joining him in the abuse of their mother" (Bancroft). Barry Goldstein, retired domestic violence attorney, batterer intervention specialist and advocate for family court reform claims that this behavior of using children and other friends and family is called domestic violence by proxy (Goldstein). This shows that when a perpetrator uses the children, that whichever way the child internalizes the witnessing of violence, he/she has been indoctrinated with fear and their own identity has been compromised.

Again, we glean some of the insidious power the partner/perpetrator has over the minds of those entirely beneath his supervision. If the power exerted over vulnerable individuals is not recognized and thwarted by friends, family, communities and churches the power and degradation over the victims increase exponentially. In most cases, women seek the counsel of their pastors first when they need help. In my own experience, there were a few individuals that could have made an impact and sought protection for us. I sought out the help of more than one minister. Doing so, however, resulted in being accused of infidelity. To my horror and dismay, they held dangerous and patriarchal beliefs, that more completely enabled the perpetrator. During one incident, the perpetrator had me crumpled on the floor while he shamed me in front of those same ministers. No one stopped him. The result was simply and tragically that I was not sufficiently submissive. Due to many ministers' toxic beliefs about the role of women and dire lack of ushering us into a safe place, these decisions put my children in great danger. The mis-use of my children and the sexual exploitation of my daughter could have been prevented. These are the words of my daughter, whose very essence and innocence were being stolen from her: "At one point during the sexual abuse he, [Dad] told me that if our home wasn't healed he might have to do the same sexual things to my sisters. He told me that I must tell no one, [especially Mother] that what he was doing was between me, him and God. I am concerned for my sisters. I am also concerned about my brother for he is now acting as my Dad's next confidant" (Cool). Lundy Bancroft points out that multiple research studies state "that a batterer is six times more likely than a non-batterer to sexually abuse his children" (Bancroft). Statistics show that half of those who are incest perpetrators also batter the children's mother. Bancroft also points out that "The overlap between domestic violence and incest is not altogether surprising to people who work with batterers and incest perpetrators because of the similarities between profiles and tactics used by the two groups" (Bancroft). Most of the time, friends, churches, family, and communities want to help. It must be understood that by the time the victims have lost a majority of their identity, they hardly have any voice left to try to obtain help. They are silenced and powerless.

Another powerful form of psychological identity theft, though not always present, is the use of God to impose and demand upon every aspect of a victim's life such that they become absorbed into a culture that eliminates individuality. Refusing to comply or leave is to risk becoming an apostate or an outcast shunned from the only life you've ever known. Your entire identity is intertwined with the group. One example of this is The Fundamentalist Church of Jesus Christ of Latter Day Saints (FLDS), a radical offshoot of the Mormon church led by a man named Warren Jeffs. His followers consider him a prophet and his mind control is exhibited through using alleged messages from God imposing upon the people how they ought to live. Often the messages from "God" merely give power to the one in control. These followers are sincere believers that have gotten bound into the group by either needing charity or they were born into it, their family history going back for generations. Anytime there is an exertion of power in an attempt to free oneself, like with Patty Hearst, or the woman who tore her photos and threw them in a drain, or a child being sexually abused, there is always a risk of escalating behavior from the perpetrator. One such woman, Carolyn Jessop, who grew intensely fearful and suffered horrible abuses inside the FLDS cult, one day secretly escaped with her children. In her autobiography, *Escape,* she is warned by a friend helping her, who knew of the power of the group, who said "Carolyn, you took the children of one of the most powerful men in the FLDS. They will hunt you down for that and plow over anyone who gets in their way. There's no way the FLDS is going to let you escape with Merril Jessop's children. This is one fight I don't think you can win." It was an intense battle to usurp Merril Jessop's iron clad control. He had "God" backing him up. Using God is a powerful weapon. Her leaving would mean most assuredly that the partner/perpetrator would be exposed, and perpetrators will do and say anything to conceal their true identity. Violence of any kind thrives in secrecy. Exposure is the greatest fear of the partner/perpetrator, so, "In order to escape accountability for his crimes, the perpetrator does everything in his power to promote forgetting. Secrecy and silence are the perpetrator's first line of defense" (Herman). Thankfully, in Carolyn Jessop's situation she escaped with her children and was given the protection that she needed. This was not the case for me and my five children. After the betrayal of church ministers the power of my partner only increased. Carolyn Jessop had an entire world looking down upon her secret community as suspicious. My secret community was me and my five children with one man using "God" as his weapon. Our family had been moved into the Vermont forests, isolated from anyone. When I left I managed to borrow twenty dollars from a woman at a thrift store to venture finding help. At that time, the indoctrination of my children was so great that they believed that "God" spoke through their father and at the end, were afraid of me. To take them with me would mean that they would sound an alarm to their father to come and get them, and then he would know where we were. My plans to find help were mostly futile. Legal advocates naturally believed my brainwashed children. My daughter once again reveals the extent of his control:

> Dad would prep us, telling us to say the 'right things' or for all of us children to get on the same page when the children's attorney, the GAL and social worker would come over to visit us. Dad convinced me to testify against my Mother in court, telling me that I was the star witness and that I could save the family and future generations if I testified. I told Dad that I did not want to. Dad's convincing ways made me believe how bad my Mother was. I believed that I was mad at her too after all that my Dad had told me about her. (Cool)

I wrote desperate letters to old friends asking them to write affidavits about my character. All my efforts to explain appeared to be an attempt in futility. I stood there, stripped of all that I was, by the power of one man. It is true that "If secrecy fails, the perpetrator attacks the credibility of his victim. If he cannot silence her absolutely, he tries to make sure that no one listens" (Herman). I lost everything.

To steal the most intimate part of a person, their identity, is one of the deepest kinds of betrayal that a human being can experience. It is the right and privilege of every human being to be safe from having their identity overpowered, interpreted, stolen, or even murdered. Judith Herman whose therapeutic experience with many escaped and traumatized victims describes the utter tragedy of someone whose life has been savaged by betrayal, the theft of identity.

> Basic trust is the foundation of belief in the continuity of life, the order of nature, and the transcendent order of the divine. In situations of terror, people spontaneously seek their first source of comfort and protection. Wounded soldiers and raped women cry for their mothers, or for God. When this cry is not answered, the sense of basic trust is shattered. Traumatized people [those who have had their identity stolen] feel utterly abandoned, utterly alone, cast out of the human and divine systems of care and protection that sustain life. Thereafter, a sense of alienation, of disconnection, pervades every relationship, from the most intimate familial bonds to the most abstract affiliations of community and religion. (Herman)

I can still remember the fragrance of my kitchen the day that I left to get help, never to return. I can remember the cold Vermont snow on my face, alone, with no one to turn to and how the betrayal by those that I was meant to trust was even colder. I can remember the pivotal points in my relationship when had I been believed by those who could have helped. I can remember falling in love at seventeen. I wonder what would have strengthened me to listen and honor my intuition and stay away from the relationship that evolved into something so horrific. It takes awareness of the problem first. Then it takes the time to encourage victims that they do not deserve to be mistreated and it takes someone to offer them safe resources to make an escape. Supportive intervention is critical. It will take intervention to educate young men that control and abuse are not acceptable. It will take churches re-evaluating the unhealthy doctrines that can become the seed beds of abuse. It will take preaching from the pulpit that abuse of any kind is wrong. It will take bravery, courage and strength to expose injustice. It will take compassion to call out the abuse and find methods to help even the perpetrators find new ways for relationship. It will take willing community effort to expose identity theft and find methods to end the generational cycles. I believe healthy relationships begin in the home, but, if that home does not know any better, then someone, needs to step up and make sure young people who are bound to fall in love at seventeen know the warning signs, before it's too late. Maybe my story will make an impact for change for the sake of future generations of families. I'm willing to apply for the job.

Works Cited

Adverse Childhood Experiences Research Study. Permanente, Kaiser.

https://www.cdc.gov/violenceprevention/acestudy/about.html.

Accessed 11 May 2017.

Bancroft, Lundy. *The Connection Between Batterers and Child Sexual Abuse*

Perpetrators. Penguin Publishing Group. Kindle Edition. 2007.

Accessed 29 Apr. 2017.

Bancroft, Lundy. *Why Does He Do That?: Inside the Minds of Angry and*

Controlling Men, Penguin Publishing Group. Kindle Edition.

Cool, Hannah. Personal Interview. April, 2017.

Goldstein, Barry. *The Quincy Solution.* 1st ed., 2014.

Herman, Judith. *Trauma and Recovery: The Aftermath of Violence – from*

Domestic Abuse to Political Terror, New York: Basic Books. 1992.

Jessop, Carolyn; Palmer, Laura. *Escape.* Crown/Archetype. Kindle

Edition.

Maiese, Michelle. "Dehumanization." *Beyond Intractability.* Eds. Guy

Burgess and Heidi Burgess. Conflict Information Consortium,

University of Colorado, Boulder. Posted: July 2003

Samsel, Michael. *Grooming.*

https://www.abuseandrelationships.org/Content/Behaviors/groo

ming.html. Accessed 11 May 2017.

Shengold, Leaonard. *Books of the Times; Destruction of Young Minds and*

Some Who Overcame. Psych Central, 1989. Accessed 29 Apr. 2017.

Is Identity Faithful?

Ty E. Ragsdale

Identity is one of the most important and defining things in the experience of being human. Identity is made up of the collection of beliefs that we hold of ourselves, and we look far and wide to fill the void that comes from not knowing who we are. Humans find their identities in a large array of things. They search for their identities in relationships, past experiences, doing good deeds, acquiring knowledge, gaining wisdom, attaining money, various substances, and to some, their faith in a higher power. The problem with identity is that it is dependent on what you put into it, and it can be changed and may not be stable. Even things that are stable can be renewed and thought of differently. They are all subject to change.

The psychological definition of identity is the qualities, beliefs, personality, looks and/or expressions that form a person (self-identity) or group (particular social category or social group). As psychologists study the brain, they have begun to decently narrow down their view on identity, and they are finding that identity is something that we can choose, but most people do not consciously choose their own identity, and instead they internalize the values of their parents and/or society (Heshmat). Identities reflect what we value the most, and people hold different identities based on what they are interested in and what activities they partake in. There are many different identities that one can have: one could be a teacher, a father, a son, a gymnast, a music lover, etc. and these things all add up to make one who he is. Adolescents are on a mad quest to find out who they really are, and often they compare their talents and skills, and see which ones to associate with. Often times, adolescents partake in risky behavior, because they are looking for acceptance among different social groups that may or may not represent them accurately. Examples include sexually risky behaviors, substance abuse for peer acceptance, etc. (IMNRC). Identity is found through trial and error, and this often includes partaking in a large array of different activities, and seeing which ones make one 'feel good." Identity is shaped over time, and taking part in risky behaviors or ones that are not actually who you are (when you have resistance to your "true self"), mentally exhausts you (Brown).

The psychological definition of identity is a great explanation of how an identity is shaped, but it doesn't answer the question of why we strain to find our identities in the first place. It also doesn't explain what happens when the facets of one's identity completely fall apart, and he is wonders "What is left?" What happens when one loses his job as a teacher? What happens if his significant other leaves? What happens when the activities and works that one does are stripped away? Is he nothing? Are their certain factors of his identity that he should prioritize over the other? What if the things that he identified with do not correspond with who he is today?

Finding one's identity is a universal journey among all humans today. The role of one's identity and what makes up one's identity largely changes depending on where you live. In the United States, our identity usually involves two things: identity to ourselves, and identity in respect to our country as a whole. Historically, this seems to have always been the case. The United States has always been a culture centered on personal freedom and choice; this has led to a largely individualistic culture. "Everyone" in the USA works to achieve their version of the "American Dream." This is usually a fantasy where the individual has lots of money, expensive cars, an attractive spouse, and maybe fame as well. Americans identify with this, and it seems that everyone wants to give the impression that they are already living the dream. Americans love hard work, and they often value their careers ahead of not only their families and friends, but often themselves as well. Americans hold the view that the busier they are, the further along with the American Dream they are. More often than not, they compete for who is the busiest. One might say, "Oh man, I got three meetings today!" and in response another might reply, "Oh yeah, well I have a meeting every day this week!" and his response would be, "Well… I was up so late for my job, that I got three hours of sleep." These kinds of boasts are not uncommon among Americans.

Another section of America's identity is found in the national identity. America's national identity is usually associated with holding values of freedom and being part of a "melting pot" of different cultures. This idea of a "melting pot" is seen as an outdated metaphor for America's hodge-podge of different cultures. Instead, we are like a kaleidoscope, where all elements come together individually in little pockets, but are distorted with one another. China Town is a good physical example of this phenomenon. They are (mostly) all Americans, inside of an American city, but with vastly different kinds of food, philosophies, and languages not considered "American" in the strictest sense. Since America also grants and supports the idea of freedom amongst its citizens, individual identities are seen to be the one with the greatest priority, unlike other cultures where there is a strong sense of communal identity, where the identity is formed based on the overall group of individuals in a community or country.

While Americans have a strong sense of national identity, our individualistic cultural identity is ultimately what decides who we are. We are the worst analyzers of our own identity, and often-times we label ourselves as something we are not. These illusions can be positive, negative, or neutral. Some people believe that they are the best at everything, that they are absolutely perfect in every way. We can venture to say that this self-analysis is not correct. Some people, however, struggle with the opposite, believing that they are the worst person in the world, that they are worthless, and that no one likes them. But if you ask a person that is close to them, they will most likely not say the same. There are also other attributes that we assign ourselves, especially in relation to tasks. I coach children's gymnastics, and I have seen with my own eyes the power of these self-analyses. I've had kids who have had flawless form, and an ability to carry out certain tasks, but some of them (especially the older kids nearing adolescent ages of 12-13) seem to develop a very "can't do" attitude. They will perform a skill that they once knew by themselves, and scream "I am bad at this" or "I can't do this" and the skill that they were working on, and their performance in my class in general seems to dramatically decline as this behavior goes by. The worst thing about these self-analysis behaviors is that often times, no amount of affirmation from others seems to change their minds. Once we have made up our minds, we have absolutely extinguished any opportunity of a renewed mind.

The next question we ask ourselves is this: "So, if I am wrong in analyzing myself, who should I listen to? Should I listen to what others have to say about me, and go with that?" Yes and no. The problem with gathering one's idea of self from others is that while his analysis of his self is often times distorted, he is the only person that experiences things in his life with his frame of reference. Simply put, the people outside of him do not experience life as he does, so he might want to take the things that they say with a grain of salt. I think that oftentimes positive attributes assigned to him from people should be taken freely, and negative attributes something to at least ponder. The problem is that if he takes what people say with complete face value, someone may say something that may completely derail him, because he is at the whim of what others say; therefore his identity is very unstable.

Sometimes it is easy to identify with one's memories, good and bad. For example, some people live their lives in "The glory days," the days from the past where "everything was amazing, and good, and perfect." Other people live their lives replaying memories of traumatic past experiences, with regrets. Robert N Kraft, professor of cognitive psychology at Otterbein University, says that oftentimes our memories, just like our self-analyses, are very distorted and sometimes fabricated based on our attitudes and influences around us. Our memories often overlap, and large generalizations are made based on who was there to

corroborate the story (Kraft). Memories are important, and they do
contribute to who one is, but one's past experiences are exactly what
they are, past *experiences*. And often times, the rose colored lenses or the
hellfire in his memories are probably inaccurate depictions of what
actually happened anyway. So his memories are not him; they are past
versions of him, reactions and behaviors manifested at a different point
of time than where he is now. One's true identity is who he is right
now, breathing in this present moment, reading this essay. His identity
is never going to be who he was. I like to think that one's present
identity is the result of his past selves getting software updates. Just
because you update Mozilla Firefox doesn't mean it changes into a
completely different program. Features get added in and bugs get
removed, and new bugs may emerge, but overall, one is, just like the
wise philosopher Big Sean once said, "...the new version of old [him]."

Now this leads to the next logical transition, because one seldom
wants to actually be who he is at this moment, so he runs away from it.
If he knows that who he is is not in the past, he will run away to the
future. It is healthy to have aspirations and goals for the future. But
let's go back to that ideal self. If one's ideal self is not acquirable, than
why does he work so hard to attain it? He will never attain it, but that
shouldn't stop him from trying. He thinks that acquiring his ideal self is
the goal, but it is the process. I have had that told to me many, many
times growing up by teachers, coaches, and parents, but what does it
mean? What it means is that although one's ideal self is never going to
be reached, the journey of getting closer to that is sweeter than actually
attaining it. Sometimes, one's ideal self is not possible to be achieved,
but sometimes he just believes that it is. He will be surprised when he

realizes that his future self is exactly what it is. It is who he *perceives as* how his identity should be and should work toward slowly evolving. This evolution of self is not always like Pokemon, where one form is changed instantaneously from one form, to the other, but more like the theoretical concept of Darwinian evolution, slow and subtle. If one places his identity in who he thinks he should be, he will always be disappointed, because he isn't that. He is himself at this given moment, breathing and reading this essay at this section of this passage, with all of his present hiccups and problems. Human beings are all like caterpillars and butterflies. They start out as caterpillars, and then they end up inside a cocoon, a cocoon of self-analysis and waiting. This cocoon can get quite comfy, but I wonder if humans are already butterflies, and they are just waiting for the right time to break free and fly, to show their marvelous and beautiful colors that they were designed to have. When is the right time? The right time is now.

Now, here is the problem about who one is in this present moment. That moment is absolutely fleeting. Every moment is different from the last. The present is constantly moving toward the future, towards the direction of time. We are always moving forward, and therefore our identities go with that movement. We are renewed and updated in even smaller increments than a milliseconds. Faster than we can even perceive. So if my identities are always changing, what is my *true* identity? If my true identity is always moving, and always changing, how can I know for certain who I am? Well, our identities aren't formed by ourselves, and they aren't formed by our actions or behaviors, from others, and even reliably by time itself. What I believe is that our identity comes from Who created us. I am not talking about my parents, although I believe that oftentimes one's parents can be a good reliable grain of salt one may take, but it is all depending on his relationship with them. I am talking about the One who has made it to where every world event, every single cosmic event, every single social interaction, the One that chose me from many sperm, the One who has decided which egg, the One that knew me before I was even born. Because if He has planned for all of these events to happen so that you would be the result, wouldn't he have known who I was going to be?

I believe that our true identities are the result of the careful planning of a Divine Creator. I think that while it is true that we ourselves navigate and try to find our identities, we are ultimately the result of God aligning every single circumstance. The beauty of this kind of identity is that no matter how I feel, no matter who tells me otherwise, the Creator gets the last say. The Creator should get the only say. I believe that since my identity is given to me by something greater than anything else, there is nothing that can derail me. I am not saying that I will never **feel** derailed, or be in a derailing circumstance, but I realize that it is not always as it seems. My identity is not always how I feel. If I feel worthless, God tells me that I am worth it. If I feel unloved, or when I cannot love myself, God tells me that I am loved. I am not addicted, I have help. Now, don't get me wrong, I still place my identity outside of this, because I *am* a gymnastics coach, I *am* still a music lover and producer, I *am* still a brother and son, I *am* still an OTC student etc. But these things don't and shouldn't get the top priority, because all of these things can be taken away in an instant.

The craziest realization of my identity was that, instead of casting all of these other sources of identity from me, when I realize that they are slowly decaying and that they can be taken from me, it makes me value them much greater. It is almost like the concept of losing one's life so that he may gain it. People die or deny you, self-medications run out, jobs can be lost, and time itself keeps moving forward endlessly and endlessly. So, I have decided that my identity is with something bigger than all of these. Everybody walks this journey called life, and I encourage us to be mindful of what we put our identities in, and ask ourselves the question: "if this was all taken away from me, who would I be?"

Works Cited

Heshmat, Sharom. "Health, Help, Happiness + Find a Therapist."

Psychology Today, Sussex Publishers, 14 Dec. 2014,

www.psychologytoday.com/. Accessed 20 Apr. 2017.

Kraft, Robert N. "What's Wrong with Inaccurate Memory?"

Psychology Today, Sussex Publishers, 30 Oct. 2014,

www.psychologytoday.com/blog/defining-

memories/201410/what-s-wrong-inaccurate-memory. Accessed 20

Apr. 2017.

"The Psychology of Adolescence." The Science of Adolescent Risk-

Taking: Workshop Report., U.S. National Library of Medicine, 1

Jan. 1970, www.ncbi.nlm.nih.gov/books/NBK53420/. Accessed

20 Apr. 2017.

Identity Contains Multitudes
Dayton Kingore

P eople can contain multitudes in multiple ways. Gut flora, bacteria, and human body cells like neurons are all present in great numbers. But the biggest factor that differentiates people is their identity, which contains multitudes as well. Identity is complicated and can be made up of many different personalities and facets. However, most do not like to think of identity this way. People think of identity as something they can control. The truth is, people have little control over their own lives. Everybody's brain is two separate hemispheres with a small bundle of neurons connecting them. This separation makes it so that it could conceivably be possible for the left and right brain to disagree about something. Because the left-brain controls speech that is the side that would usually win. People also have no choice in whether their brain functions correctly or not. Mental illnesses can become serious, notably with dissociative identity disorder. These sufferers have no choice in the shocking development of their second identity. Even something as simple as sleepwalking can change personality dramatically. Many people do not realize these changes can occur or manifest an identity. Furthermore, these changes are unexpected and out of their hands. More people need to realize that their identity is fluid and sometimes just one identity living among others. That way they can come to expect changes and be more prepared for them. Everybody has a bad day sometimes but occasionally that bad day can mean a little more than usual. When they feel compelled to do something out of the ordinary like act very aggressive, they can stop and really look at what they are doing. This can have multiple effects: it can cause them to look more closely at their actions, or to look more closely at personal identity. If they can think of all the attributes they would apply to themselves as their identity and remember those distinctions, they can better protect themselves from identity change or the prevalence of a different identity. However, the existence of other identities is not necessarily a bad thing. That may be a natural part of the human experience. It can be good to grow, change, and adapt to new things, identity among them.

To better identify what it looks like for a person to have more than one identity, the definition of identity must be stated. There can be many different definitions based on the context. For example, the dictionary definition would be: "the condition of being oneself or itself, and not another" (Identity). That would be a satisfactory definition in certain contexts. In this context, it will be defined as the beliefs, personality, and expressions that make a person. Using this definition will make it much easier to know what qualities make up an identity. Having multiple identities does not mean literally having two or more separate identities like dissociative identity disorder. It means simply that other identities could be identified based on various human behaviors.

Walt Whitman wrote that we "contain multitudes" (Whitman). He was not a scientist or psychologist, but he was an amazing author, poet, and intellectual mind. His beliefs coincide with the thoughts of many psychologists. The most obvious and pronounced example of a human exhibiting multiple personalities is dissociative identity disorder or DID (Kluft). Dissociation is something that many people experience every day, such as in daydreaming or getting lost in a song, but this disorder is a much more serious form of dissociation. DID is characterized by the DSM-5 (Diagnostic and Statistical Manual of Mental Disorders, 5th Edition) as "a disruption of identity characterized by two or more distinct personalities" (Association 292). The personalities will have different memories, thoughts, and a completely different sense of identity. The identities can be a different sex, age, race, or even different postures or ways of talking. This disorder is mostly caused by severe physical and sexual abuse during childhood as sufferers often have a history of abuse in their childhood (Bell, Jacobson and Fox). The existence of dissociative identity disorder is an intense topic with many psychologists who say it is an offshoot of borderline personality disorder. Much of a DID sufferer's second identity will be determined by the kind of culture they live in. Often religious sufferers will manifest their other identity as a demon or spirits. This has led to some believing that DID is not its own disorder, but a symptom of another disorder like borderline personality disorder (Association 296). Whether that is true or not does not change the fact that these people have more than one identity.

Using the above definition of identity, they experience different thoughts between identities, they believe different things about themselves and about the world, and they will exhibit different expressions between personalities. However, this is considered a rare condition with prevalence being somewhere between 1.4 and 1.6 percent (Association 223). That is far less than the general population and thus cannot confirm the idea that many people can exhibit multiple personalities.

A much more common example of another identity would be somnambulism, commonly called sleepwalking. The existence of another personality is not nearly as distinct as with dissociative identity disorder, but it can still be found. Consider the idea that when sleepwalking, the person is exhibiting an entirely different personality as opposed to just performing complex behaviors while asleep. To use the definition of identity, the sleepwalker will have thoughts atypical to their own identity. They will say things that make little sense. They will sometimes not know where they are or recognize the people around them. Sometimes they do dangerous things like cooking or driving at odd hours in the night (Association 399). These are all behaviors and thoughts they do not usually have. They will often have an unrecognizable look on their face, they walk or hold their body in strange positions, and they can become scared or violent quickly (Association 400). Sleepwalkers have even killed people in rare cases (Hurham). Again, these are signs that they are not behaving per their normal identity. The sleepwalker is unaware of things happening around them. They will often think that a closet or a dresser is a toilet, indicating that the identity does not know what a toilet looks like. This all means that a sleepwalker is psychologically abnormal.

How could it be that sleepwalking could be considered a separate identity? The brain could give a good explanation of this. When going to sleep, the brain is going through many complicated stages scientists still do not have a complete understanding of. Sleep technically starts in bundles of cells of the hypothalamus in the brainstem. The cells will start slow wave sleep or SWS. It is after SWS starts that consciousness is lost (Health). This is where what is called N3 sleep takes place, and where sleepwalking occurs (Blaivas). N3 sleep is when the body heals and repairs itself, usually lasting between 45 to 90 minutes. During N3 sleep, delta brain waves are produced with a frequency of about .5 to 4 Hz. This is different from awake brain waves which are usually gamma or beta waves anywhere from 12 to 100 Hz (School). Though the brain remains highly active during sleep, it behaves differently. In addition to the slow brain waves, the prefrontal cortex will also have a high voltage compared to other regions (School). The two neuroscientists who originally studied the prefrontal cortex called it the "mental sketchpad" (Arnsten). It largely controls personality, thoughts, and emotions which are all key components of identity. The changes in the prefrontal cortex during sleep are pronounced enough to discern that a sleepwalker is exhibiting a different identity, though this too is a condition that is only experienced by a small percentage of the population. That small percentage is also almost always made up of children who eventually grow out of it. This does indicate that some people can exhibit other personalities without suffering from a serious mental illness.

Finally, it's clear that the brain itself can contain multiple identities. Every person has two hemispheres of their brain connected by their corpus callosum. The corpus callosum is a bundle of nerves that connects the two hemispheres and allows them to communicate. The left hemisphere of the brain is responsible for controlling the right side of the body along with language, numbers, and other functions. The right side of the brain is responsible for controlling the left side of the body along with spatial awareness, musical awareness, and facial recognition among other functions. This is how the two halves function with most brains but some behave differently.

The specialization of the two hemispheres is purposeful and designed so that work is spread more equally throughout the brain. Because the two parts of the brain perform separate tasks, information between the two hemispheres must be shared so the hemispheres can make decisions with data gathered by both hemispheres. The corpus callosum is the only thing connecting the two parts of the brain and its main purpose is to share information. In the past, patients with severe epilepsy would have their corpus callosum severed to stop the spread of epilepsy from one hemisphere to the other (Fitsiori, Nguyen and Karentzos). This succeeds in stopping the spread of epilepsy but also causes some interesting behaviors.

Neuroscientists Roger Sperry and Michael Gazzaniga conducted experiments to learn more about this phenomenon which they dubbed split-brain. They found that people with split-brain behave mostly normal. They can play sports, walk, talk, read, and do just about anything they could before they had the surgery. However, they could not learn behaviors that required independent movement by both hands, such as playing the piano. To conduct tests on split-brain subjects, the doctors used what is called a tachistoscope to show different visuals to each eye. This would allow them to only show a picture to the right or left hemisphere (Media). For a simple explanation, if a split-brain subject named Alex were to participate in one of their experiments, he would sit down and stare at a dot in the middle of a screen. A dog would flash to the right of the dot and Alex would be asked what flashed on the screen. He would reply immediately that he had seen a dog. Remember that Alex's right eye would see the dog which would make the information go to the left hemisphere. The left hemisphere controls language which allows him to say that he had seen a dog. If a spoon was flashed on the left side, Alex would say that he had seen nothing. The scientists would then ask Alex to pick out an object that he thinks might have flashed and he would pick a spoon every time. Alex's left brain did not see the original flash of the spoon and thus he was not able to say that he had seen a spoon. His right brain saw the spoon, but the right brain does not control language and because his right brain cannot communicate with his left, he said he saw nothing. The right brain could only communicate through Alex's left hand.

This an interesting phenomenon indicates that the left and right brain are two separate entities that work together and act as one. The two hemispheres have their own specializations, they perform different functions, and they have their own ways of communicating. When they cannot talk to each other, they get confused. In the second experiment, if asked why he chose a spoon, Alex would make up a response. The left brain missed key information from the right brain so it would be forced to decide on a response based on the information it had. The two hemispheres express themselves differently, one through speech and the other nonverbally. The two hemispheres are like two supercomputers connected by a few wires. They do a lot of their own specialized computing, but they also rely on each other to process certain information. They are two separate computers, but they are part of one network.

Identity is fluid and ever changing. It can be easily compared to the way a river changes a landscape. Sometimes the river will decide to turn and divert course. Sometimes the river will decide to fork or go underground. An identity is not some sacred monolith. It is the relationship between many different physical and psychological parts of the body. It decides the type of response the body gives when something unexpected happens. The examples of DID, sleepwalking, and split-brain are just that—examples. They exist among many things that change or add to identity. They are somewhat contributed to by outside forces, but they mostly manifest themselves from within. This means that there are thousands of other things from outside and within that change or add to identity.

Works Cited

Arnsten, Amy F. T. "Stress Signalling Pathways That Impair Prefrontal
  Cortex Structure and Function." Nature Reviews (2009): 422. Web.
  19 April 2017.
  <https://www.ncbi.nlm.nih.gov/pmc/articles/PMC2907136/#>.

Association, American Psychiatric. Diagnostic and Statistical Manual of
  Mental Disorders. Vol. 5. Arlington: American Psychiatric
  Publishing, 2013. 5 vols. 19 April 2017.
  <https://psicovalero.files.wordpress.com/2014/06/dsm-v-
  manual-diagnc3b3stico-y-estadc3adstico-de-los-trastornos-
  mentales.pdf>.

Bell, Hope, et al. The Role of Religious Coping and Resilience in
  Individuals With Dissociative Identity Disorder. 2014. 19 April
  2017.

Blaivas, Allen J. "Sleepwalking." 13 April 2015. MedlinePlus. 19 April
  2017.

Fitsiori, A, et al. "The Corpus Callosum: White Matter or Terra
  Incognita." The British Journal of Radiology (2011): 18. Web. 19
  April 2017.
  <https://www.ncbi.nlm.nih.gov/pmc/articles/PMC3473808/>.

Health, National Institutes of. "Brain Basics: Understanding Sleep."
  n.d. National Institute of Neurological Disorders and Stroke. 19
  April 2017.

Hurham. Joseph Mitchell Fond Not Guilty in 'Sleepwalking' Murder
  Trial. 2015.

"Identity." n.d. Merriam-Webster. 19 April 2017.

Kluft, Richard P. Dissociative Identity Disorder. Ed. Larry K. Michelson and Williams J. Ray. 1996. 19 April 2017. <https://link.springer.com/chapter/10.1007/978-1-4899-0310-5_16>.

Media, Nobel. "The Split Brain Experiments." 2014. Nobelprize.org. Web. 19 April 2017.

School, Division of Sleep Medicine at Harvard Medical. "Healthy Sleep." 18 December 2007. Natural Patterns of Sleep. 19 April 2017.

Whitman, Walt. Leaves of Grass. 9 vols. Walt Whitman, 1855.

Identity Crisis

Kathleen Ruffell

We as humans tend to believe we have a grip on our identity. We like to think we know who we are on the inside and out. But what if a person you know suddenly starts slipping in a direction you no longer recognize and they start to lose the identity you once knew? What if they start to have a short temper with others, and they get anxious and overwhelmed over the slightest events in life? What if they like to be alone, and they start feeling empty inside even though you have surrounded them with a positive, supporting and happy environment? Why would this happen to someone who, up until a certain point, seemed to be just fine? This is exactly what happened to my daughter so I began researching all the possibilities as to why her identity suddenly changed. After much research, I think I may have come across several possibilities for the sudden change. Out of the many implausible ideas out there such as Sigmund Freud's psychosexual theory, bullying, and even astrology, I believe I have found some plausible options for why my daughter's identity has dramatically changed.

My beautiful daughter grew up in loving and supportive household. My husband and I have been together since high school and we have a strong and happy relationship. We are easy going and do not allow negative people or negative activities to surround our household. We don't worry about the small things in life and help each other out as much as possible. I say we are very fortunate, because we don't have to work at our marriage. There is never any arguing or fighting. We just don't see a reason for it. We relax, have fun, and treat each other with respect.

My daughter was a delightful, well-behaved, open-hearted, happy little girl. She was almost never sad or had any temper tantrums like most kids do at that age. I can't ever remember her being unhappy with anything that she experienced. Everyone was always quick to lend a hand at babysitting because she would always bring a smile and lighten up their day. She was never any trouble.

I started to notice, however, that as she got into her teenage years, things started to change. She was starting to get short tempered towards me and her closest friends. It seemed like things started to overwhelm her when she was faced with multiple things at once. She was hateful on the inside and displayed that hate on the outside as well. I figured it was just teenage hormones that she was going through, but as she got older, things seemed like they got worse instead of better. It's hard to believe that a child who grew up in such a loving, positive environment could turn out this way. So, the first thing I researched was Sigmund Freud's psychosexual theory. This theory has some interesting perspectives on how a child's identity is developed.

Freud believed that one's personality is developed through a series of psychosexual stages that are determined by a small child's sexuality development. According to Freud, each stage occurs at a specific time in a child's life. If one becomes fixated on any of these stages, that person can develop certain personality traits that can be tied back to that stage in life. During these stages, different erogenous zones, or different areas of the body that produce pleasurable feelings, are important because they can become the source of unresolved conflict (Ciccarelli and White 412). Conflicts that are not resolved can result into getting fixated to some level of degree of development. This can lead to a child that will grow into adulthood carrying emotional unresolved issues that can then lead to other emotional diseases. The theory includes the following stages. Oral, anal, and phallic.

The first stage is the oral stage, which is developed within the first 18 months of life. A child that is taken off the bottle or the mom's breast too early or even too late and made to learn how to drink from a cup can later be connected to that child having health issues. These health problems can include overeating, drinking too much, excessive smoking, talking too much, or even being too dependent and optimistic or too aggressive and pessimistic (Ciccarelli and White 412). I followed the board of pediatrics suggestions with my daughter along with what cues she was giving me and when it came time to wean, she had no issue with transitioning from the bottle to a cup.

The second stage is the anal stage. This is believed to start between the ages of 18 to 36 months. Freud thinks that as the child becomes a toddler, the erogenous zone moves from the mouth to the anus. He also believed that children got a great deal of pleasure from both withholding and releasing their feces whenever they want to, leading him to label this the anal stage. He, of course, is talking about toilet training and the fascination that children find in having control over what they produce. Freud suggests that when toilet training a toddler, if the demand for learning is too harsh, then this could result in a child who will openly refuse to go when asked and could further translate into the adult as having an anal, explosive personality. This personality will generally display destructive and hostile personalities. My daughter at times now can display destructive personalities when she gets to that tipping point of drowning in self-sorrow, not toward others but to herself. Once again, however, she never had any difficulty with being toilet trained. She loved the idea of being independent and made those decisions mostly on her own.

The third stage is called the phallic stage which happens between 3 and 6 years old. Freud states that this is when the erogenous zone shifts to the genitals. This is the stage when boys and girls start to realize that they have different body parts than their opposite sex. This stage centers on "the awakening sexual feelings of the child" (Ciccarelli and White 414). According to Freud, little girls develop what is known as an Electra Complex. This is when girls see "their father as the target of their affections and their mother as the rival" (Ciccarelli and White 414). It's when the father encourages the sexual attraction back that a fixation can occur. This fixation can lead to immature sexual attitudes as an adult.

My daughter went through a stage when she was in love with my husband. And he would always put her first over me, just because it was the cute thing to do to make her feel like she was superior. He would do things like go to open the door for me, then on purpose say to me out loud in front of her "Excuse me ma'am, I want my beautiful little lady to go first," and let her go through the door first. This would make her smile so big to know that I came second to her. Now that my daughter is grown up, she has no problems or issues with dating people her own age or her sexual orientation. So, I find it hard to believe Freud's theory of the stages of personality development. None of these seemed to explain my daughter's mental issues. That led me to look elsewhere for explanations, and the next theory I researched was developed hundreds of years before Freud even came along. This would be the concepts behind astrology.

Now I already know that there are many people that do not want to believe this farfetched concept at all, but one needs to take a moment to look at the close relations and similarities of this ancient way of thinking. I would have never of given any thought that my daughter's mental illness had anything to do with her zodiac sign but let me try explain. According to Lauren Kassel, a professor at the University of Cambridge's Department of History and Philosophy of Science, "Medical Astrology, or iatromathematics, stretches as far back as the field of medicine itself and is one of the longest standing intellectual traditions on the planet" (Wolfson 2). In the article, it states that the season of your birth appears to have a strong influence on what your life will be like in the future. Depending on whether you were born in the spring, summer, fall, or winter, you could have a higher rate of developing mental disorders like schizophrenia, depression, sleep disorders and even allergies. (Wolfson 3). Even though it is a bit tough to understand, Chris Ciarleglio, a neuroscientist from Brown University, admits that there is a connection between seasonal birth and certain disorders.

A few years back, a team of researchers from the McMahon lab at Vanderbilt University did a study to satisfy the advocates of the scientific method along with astrologers. The researchers put mice into three different environments, each one corresponding to a different photoperiod of the year: one a 12-hour spilt light and dark environment to represent the spring and fall; one 18 light to 6 dark, to represent the summer; and finally one 6 to 18 to represent the winter. After 21 days, the researchers took the mice and moved them to different photoperiod environments to see how they would adjust. Most of the mice did just fine, with one big exception. The mice of the winter months displayed mood instability and rapid change of emotions (Wolfson 4). These mood instabilities could be a lack of vitamin D that the body needs to produce serotonin. If the body produces low serotonin, this can lead to depression (Gaynor). This study correlates correctly with my daughter's birth month which is in January, which might explain some of her vulnerability to depression and anxiety.

Another article, by Dr. Suzel Fuzuau-Braesch, a biologist from the University of Paris, found that astrologists have believed that that are two points on the horoscope wheel that were of great importance. That is the ascendant and the mid heaven. The ascendant is the point where the ecliptic, the point where sun crosses the sky, crosses the eastern horizon. The mid heaven is the high point of the sun's apparent path where the ecliptic intersects the prime meridian. Astrologers believe that a planet within a few degrees of either point will influence the personality of anyone who happens to be born at that time. For over 23 years, Michel Gauquelin, a graduate in statistics and psychology from Sorbonne did studies backing up this belief of the effects of Venus, the Moon, Jupiter and Saturn. The effects of these planets were the same of what astrologers found. During one of his studies he followed fifteen different dog breeds to insure the results were not specific to that breed with a total of one hundred litters equaling 500 puppies over a period of five years. The breeders had no knowledge the study was being done on astrology. The results exceeded the threshold of significance of the personality traits that correlated with the planets. The puppies with Mars and Jupiter at the angles were more aggressive and extroverted and the puppies with an Angular Moon displayed calm and friendly demeanors (Robert 542). Even though many scientists are skeptical about your horoscope relating to mental illness, personally it has made me wonder a bit more about the role it can play. However, one theory I am a little bit more certain about is how an injury could lead to the onset a mental illness.

My daughter was very involved in athletics during middle school and into the start of high school. During an intense soccer tournament, she was running down the field trying to get the ball from the opposing team and the other player kicked the ball at point blank straight into her head. The force was so powerful that it knocked her unconscious. We had to take her to the emergency room. They kept her for a few hours and they ran a CAT scan to see if she had suffered a concussion. According to the website Science Nordic, Danish scientists have discovered that if you suffer from a serious head trauma such as a fractured skull or a concussion, your risk for developing certain mental disorders could increase by over 400 percent. This information was based on a study on all Danes born between 1977 and 2000, totaling 1.4 million people. These people were followed until 2010. During this period, there was a total of 113,906 that had been to the emergency room for head injuries. Out of those patients, it showed that 65 percent were more likely to be diagnosed with schizophrenia, 59 percent more likely to develop depression, 28 percent more likely to be diagnosed with bipolar disorder and an entire 439 percent more likely to suffer from organic mental disorders (Hansen).

You might question the idea that maybe this mental disease might have always been there and maybe just didn't express itself until after the injury by coincidence. Dr. Orlovska believes there are several reasons a severe head injury can bring on mental disorders. One is that the head injuries "can destroy a certain area of the brain. This damage can lead to the development of a mental disorder. An injury like a concussion has shown to affect the neurotransmitters that the brain uses to communicate with the nervous system, and when this is disrupted it causes an imbalance that is shown to be associated with the development of mental health issues" (Hansen). After my daughter had been evaluated by the emergency room doctor, he dismissed the chances of any type of head injury. A few months after this happened I started to notice a change in my daughter. Could it have been from the force hit to the head? Or was it just the typical emotional changes most teenagers go through?

I started to notice my daughter was being short tempered toward the family and close friends. She wanted to be left alone in her room, which was not like her normal outgoing attitude. We would fight almost every morning when I was getting her up for school because I would have to go in her room several times to wake her up and she would tell me she was too tired to go to school. I figured she was just being lazy so I would tell her that she had no choice but to get herself together and get ready. This went on for months. Finally, one day, I got a call from the school saying that a girl twice her size came up from behind her and knocked her to the ground and started kicking her in the ribs and back while hitting her with her fist. She was hurt bad enough to take her to the urgent care to make sure her ribs had not been broken. This was traumatic for her as one could imagine. Not only did this happen, it happened in the hall in between classes for half the school to see. It turned out this bullying had been going on through her freshman, sophomore and some of her junior year.

So how does bullying affect the mental health? According to the National Institute of Child Health and Human Development, bullying "can lead to physical injury, social problems, emotional problems, and even death. Children and adolescents who are bullied are at increased risk for mental health problems, including depression, anxiety, headaches, and problems adjusting to school. Bullying also can cause long-term damage to self-esteem" (www.nichd.nih.gov). I whole heartedly agree with this statement. My daughter's grades started to drop, she lost most of her friends, and she no longer wanted to compete in any type of school sports, which I knew killed her soul because she was so good at them and loved to compete.

This has been a heartbreaking struggle for us as a family. Our once fun-loving daughter has now become a lost, sad, unstable, irritable person. Over the years as she has now grown into adulthood, she still struggles with mental illness. Some days are better than others, but she still breaks down and gets overwhelmed and frustrated very easily. She has been under the care of a psychiatrist for four years now. None of them has given us a definite answer as to why this is now such a struggle for her. The professionals explain to us that it could be a number of things. One even told us that her brain was still young and she just needed to grow up and get tough. But by doing this independent research on my own, I now have a better understanding of the possibilities of how a mental illness can develop and change one's identity.

Works Cited

Ciccarelli, Sandra., and Noland White. Psychology an Exploration: 3rd
    Edition. United States. 2015.

Gaynor, Rachell. Accuweather: "Does Rainy Fall Weather Really Affect
    Your Brain Mood?". April 13, 2015. Web

Hansen, Malene. Science Nordic: "Head Injury Can Cause Mental
    Illness." Jan 3, 2014. Web.

National Institute of Child Health and Human Development. "How
    does bullying affect health and well-being?" Web. n.d.

Marks, Robert. Journal of Scientific Exploration. Vol 23. Issue 4. Web.
    Winter. 2009.

Wolfson, Elijah. The Atlantic. "Your Zodiac Sign, Your Health". Web.
    Nov 15. 2013.

A Question a Day Keeps the War Away

David Vergel de Dios

The State, which can be defined as a sovereign land mass, has influence over the ideals, mindset, and direction of the people who reside within its jurisdiction. The State can have a profound impact on an individual's identity. The colonists of Britain living in the New World were not being treated with hostile actions unfit for living, but they were told that a tyrant was swindling away all their money, though a British citizen in England was paying far more in taxes. The people of Germany during the 1930s and 1940s were not evil people. However, they were told by their leaders that their nation needed to return to its previous glory. Both examples are prime case studies of how powerful of an effect the State has on an individual's identity.

The identity of an individual can be affected by the State in four main ways. First, the governing body, through the leaders and media, affect the identity with their forced agenda. Second is how the individual chooses to respond to their government. The individual could respond to their governing body by accepting, refusing, or forming a new independent idea. The third way comes from understanding the importance of governing influence. Germany will be the negative example of the danger of government influence and the American Revolution will represent the positive power. Lastly will be the Socratic Method and how the world of today could be set up for prosperity by individuals with an inner drive for improvement of the State through question and reasoning.

To begin, the head of every monument is usually the face of a leader who is worth remembering or who demands to be remembered. These individuals tend to have some of the greatest impact on the lives of those who live under them. Leaders of nations have many powers that can form the opinion and overall sphere of mind that a nation takes on. They can also talk the people of a State into a frenzy or into a productive State of mind. Martin Luther King Jr. accomplished the latter, while dictators have been known to do the opposite to obtain power. Leaders have always been able to communicate to the masses, from large public gatherings to the emergence of the media. Individuals will stand behind a leader they like, and the values they support. As a leader embraces ideas, such as religious tolerance or ethnic diversity, the same can be said for the people. These States will likely have a diverse work force spanning a horizontal and vertical plane, meaning that people of all races or religions have the opportunity to work low or moderate paying jobs with an equal chance to rise to an educated, executive position. Leaders with tolerance will yield individuals with tolerance.

Media in a State is another powerful way to gather individuals into a single State of mind. If a piece of government propaganda is circulated throughout the vast avenues of the media, communities emerge with rallies as seen during the Obama administration (2008-2016). Pro-gun companies organized these rallies, where they called out citizens who were told that their rights were in jeopardy. Whether any rights were at risk did not matter; what really mattered was the number of individuals who responded. There was a calling, an influencing of people, for a cause. Looking at Germany in the 1930s, there was a "return to greatness" that the government pushed. The media has a powerful influence on the individuals of a State, so much so that when needed, the State itself hears the outcry. The parallel from the individual's identity and the media's influence is that of personal placement (where one decides his or her own allegiance). A question asked by the individual as he or she assesses the justness of a cause "Do I identify with this message? Do I care enough about it to participate?" These questions can lead to the solidifying of a one's values within his or her identity.

The media can be seen as a coin with mainstream media on one side and social media on the other. Unlike mainstream media, social media is a way for the people to have their own say and spread their ideas. Social media gives people the power to discuss issues within their State and, in best case scenarios, come up with a solution that can be presented to the governing party via petition. Unfortunately, social media is seldom that productive. Most people would rather share photos of their latest meal than chose to recognize issues of importance. Social media is a powerful tool when used for a cause. When utilized, it allows the subjects of a State to address the fallacies or to agree upon established legislation.

From stimulus there is response, and there are three steps of response when looking at an individual and the State influence. The first step is the individual agreeing with the influence. When an individual agrees with his State, there is further production of ideas and values. Progress, whether positive or negative, can be made when all parts of a State are on board. When individuals accept what they are told, they expect to be truthfully informed. With the leader/leaders, media, and social media all influencing the identity of an individual, it may be easiest for the individual to just smile and nod their head "yes." In both Nazi Germany and the American Revolution, this rang true. Citizens in Hitler's Germany were ridiculed and thought enemies of the State if they did not accept the truth the masses had bought into. The same goes for those who stood against the ideals of the revolution in Colonial America. Pressure was put on as a slogan coined by American Revolutionaries came out: "Join, or Die." Not a lot more truth could be packaged up in three words.

Problems arise in the second step of response, when individuals begin to refute the influence of the State. The people begin to tear apart from each other when some see through what they are being force-fed. Plato's Allegory of the Cave is a perfect example of seeing the bigger picture. The idea is of one who leaves the dark cave, which is void of free thinking, where the only information is spoon-fed. Outside the cave is where the identity of individuals is tested and where that question of "Do I identify with this message, and do I care enough about it to participate?" becomes far more dangerous. Leaving the cave, or bombardment of forced influence, is a matter of opening the eyes of the people to the world around them. Fact checking against non-biased sources just might be the act of leaving the cave. Leaving the void is easy; the difficult endeavor comes with liberating others, and the impossible arises with destroying the cave altogether. The act of becoming informed and starting to look at the State objectively, with a mindset to better it, is a true test of one's identity.

The first two steps have laid the ground work. The last step of response is forming innovative ideas and new opinions. This step may be most prevalent and easily accomplished in States with unrestricted free speech. However, refuting the State may be a capital crime elsewhere. There are many dangers when forming new ideas. Thousands of would-be influential free thinkers have been extinguished before their prime due to fearful repercussions. It is the rejecting individuals who have paved the way for change. The identity of those influenced by the State are those who are complacent, expecting change to arise by way of someone else. The identity of those who refuse forced information become stronger. They are the up-and-coming leaders who the fearful rely upon to change unfavorable conditions or legislation. How one identifies after leaving the cave can have an unfavorable impact upon a population. One could identify as a patriot, accepting the information of the State and going to battle for the cause of the nation, or one could identify as a patriot who goes to battle for a cause in rejection of one nation and in favor of a new.

American Colonists saw all parts of the response to influence. First, they had a leader who chose money and power before his people. They saw a legislation that they did not favor, like the Quartering Act of 1765 and as the Stamp Act of 1765. These were not the first steps of the response process; they were the second. The first step came by way of the French and Indian War, where the colonists had taken up arms with the British army to fight. The war was the accepting of information, because the colonists were attacked and had to rely on the British for aid. The rejection came when the colonists were forced to house and provide provisions for British soldiers after the war. Along with soldier provisions, taxes were placed on everyday items and small luxuries like playing cards and dice (Quartering Act).

With the colonists up in arms, they had to not only pay back Britain colonial expenses for the war, but also had to house troops responsible for ensuring the debts be paid. They entered the final stage of response. They refuted the legislation and ideas placed upon them, and substituted them with their own. A Declaration of Independence was sent to the English governing body as a petition of the people for their own jurisdiction. A swift reprimand was set in place and a war erupted due to the influence of a State on its subjects. Powerful is the identity of the people when they rally behind a cause and are backed into a corner.

The opposite side of the same coin is the German people and their romantic fantasy of return to their former glory. Germany had lost out during the First World War, being forced to pay back reparations in substantial amounts from a war they did not start, but intended to win. The people of Germany were much like those of Colonial America; they were being forced to pay sums of money and had restrictions placed upon them, limiting their power. When individuals from a country like Germany (built by military conquest) had their faces rubbed in a loss of life, land, and might, they tried to identify with previous power. The world seemed too busy with their own issues to see that Germany had started to militarize yet again. The difference between Germany and Colonial America was that Germany had no one paying attention to them when a young war veteran began to influence his people.

Hitler was asked by the government to spy on a work party; he took it over and his ascension to power began (Tonge). As popularity of the Nazi party rose in Germany, there was no large resistance to the ideas of a young and ambitious Hitler. With a distrust for the current party who had surrendered during the First World War, Hitler chose to renew the glory of Germany through conquest. His identity before taking power is important to observe to understand the mindset he pushed on people. He had felt betrayed by his country at the surrender to the allies and he was going to avenge the country which he held dear. Hitler and his Germany went through the same steps as the American Colonists. However, their difference relies on their direction and the observer. The identity of the State of Germany relied on a radical idealist. This caused the people to blame their hardship on another group instead of the leadership that brought them to a State of turmoil.

Lastly, with history best left in the past, the question of "What lies ahead?" must be asked. The current standing of the world seems to be in the first stage of the influence response, indicating that it is an ongoing cycle. The cycle will continue to repeat until questioning all information is a natural human habit. Plato's mentor and close friend, Socrates, developed what would be called the Socratic Method. The very definition is "…asking continual questions until a contradiction [is] exposed…" (Prospective Students). Socrates understood the importance of not knowing every answer and finding out that others did not know either. From there, we begin to form theories, statements that have not yet had a question asked that disproved them. The Socratic Method is important to the influence of the State on an individual's identity because one should never blindly accept an answer. We do not develop and prosper because we accept without questioning, but rather because we ask questions until we prove something undeniably true.

The Socratic Method should be utilized by individuals within a State so that State influence does not alter the individual's identity in a negative way. Life today is far faster moving than in previous generations. News can be seen through a screen on the train ride to work and a revolutionary idea can be spread from a coffee shop. With so much information so easily accessible, it is drastically important, now more than ever, to stay informed and on top of what is truth. One should avoid blindly accepting ideas that are pushed to the masses. Today, individual identity is at risk due to the amount of influence available from the State. The first phase of the influence response cycle seems to be taking place currently where complacent mindsets wait for free thinkers to vocalize new ideas. Today, the States are circulating the latest religious intolerance and racial division with new headlines hourly. Maybe a State is easier to control when it is divided and in turmoil. The American Colonies were united with a single cause and fought under a unified flag. Contrary to this, Germans turned on each other and blamed other groups for their misfortune, resulting in their ultimate demise.

To close, people of this day and age could set future generations up for a successful and peaceful second and third stage of influence response. Citizens should start asking their leaders for a variety of accurate information. Media should strive to inform people rather than be concerned about how well their pockets are lined, with no regard to the affect they have on the division of a State. Social media should advocate for individuals to come up with solutions to a State's current issues, and the government should allow the idea to be presented to them once a problem is tactfully answered. The technology of today gives the world the ability to ask a whole new set of questions with a depth yet unseen. Question even this information and form an opinion about it, for that is the true nature of starting a conversation for change. The Socratic Method is the door handle to a whole new world. We as a people just need to open it.

Works Cited

"Quartering Act." U.S. History. Quartering Act (1765). U-s-
history.com, n.d. Web. 25 Apr. 2017.

"The Socratic Method." Prospective Students. The Socratic Method |
University of Chicago Law School. University of Chicago Law
School, n.d. Web. 25 Apr. 2017.

Tonge, Stephen. "Hitler: The Rise to Power." *European History*. A Web
of English History, Jan. 2016. Web. 25 Apr. 2017.

The Self: Illusion, Perception, Deception

Hannah Quick

The core self is a crucial concept to most of us. We spend time examining the self. We may endeavor to stay true to self. We all want to know what our true self is, so we search. We search for the meaning of self in philosophy, in psychology, in neuroscience, and inside our own consciousness. But we can never truly know ourselves. All that we find when we look for the self is a flawed interpretation of who we are that we perceive as a core identity. Yet even this illusion can play an important role in our lives.

What is the self? Self is a core, essential quality that makes you who you are, something without which you could not still be you. The self can be conceptualized as an element of the mind. The aspect of the mind that makes it distinctly you is some important pattern or way of thinking characteristic of you. The things that people describe when speaking of the self — such as culture, nature, and nurture — are all considered part of self because they in some way contribute to thinking patterns.

If you are your consistent views and ways of thinking, then to know yourself, you need to be able to view your own thoughts objectively. However, the very idea that you could separate yourself from your self to think impartially on your own thoughts is something of a conundrum. This inability to view our own consciousness from a detached standpoint is one of the reasons to believe we can never attain true self-knowledge.

Another reason to discount our capacity for self-knowledge is the possibility that the quality of self, the way we generally think of it, is nonexistent. If self does not exist, the issue of self-knowledge becomes even more complicated, since we could only evaluate a perception of an imagined quality. While initially it may seem strange to suggest that you do not have a self, there are actually sound, logical reasons to discount the idea of an essential quality of self.

By definition, self is a quality such that it is who you are, and you are not who you are without it. Consequently, if you can alter your mental features without altering self, the mind cannot be the self. It follows, then, that in order for the self to exist, it must be temporally consistent to be essential to the selfhood. If the mind were the essential component of self, then in order for you to have a self that exists through time, the basic patterns of the mind must remain consistent throughout your lifetime. However, this is not the case.

While it's difficult to examine the unity of the mind through time, research indicates that many of our important mental characteristics can change drastically. The two major components of our thinking are *what we think* and *how we think* — or, more simply, beliefs and personality. While you might expect that these factors are fairly permanent, both are in fact fluid.

According to a recent longitudinal study that followed individuals from the age of 14 to 77, personality transforms "beyond recognition" across lifetime. Participants completed a questionnaire on personality that addressed six personality characteristics: "self-confidence, perseverance, stability of moods, conscientiousness, originality, and desire to learn" (Goldhill). The researchers had expected that personality would be stable over the 63 years, because previous studies had found evidence of the consistency of personality traits over shorter periods of time. However, they concluded, "our correlations did not support this hypothesis" (Goldhill).

Not only is personality highly mutable, but research also indicates that, "even our deepest convictions can be manipulated by simple trickery." In another study, researchers surveyed volunteers' attitudes on "everything from internet privacy to the Middle East conflict" (Burkeman). Researchers then asked participants to review and discuss their answers. However, researchers changed the questions so that participants' answers were the opposite of what they had originally stated. The majority of people were "perfectly willing to argue for the opposite of at least one position they'd originally taken" (Burkeman), indicating that their "real" opinions were not as important as what they thought their opinions had been in the past.

As demonstrated by the research, your original mental self does not persist through time. If mental self does not persist, it does not exist, because if you can lose your unique style of thinking without losing your selfhood, then the mind is not the self. Consequently, whoever you are now, you are eventually going to be someone quite different.

The lack of identity consistency over time implies an absence of personal continuity. Obviously, whether we defined an individual at one time as the same person at another time would depend on how much a person could change and still be the same person. If you do not have the same self, for instance, as a teenager and a senior, how far can the concept extend? It could also be true that the teenager and the middle-aged individual are not the same self. If we continued to progressively smaller intervals of time, and found that in each case, the self at a time A was never the same at a time B arbitrarily close to time A, the following conclusion is that the mind is slightly different at every moment. In a sense, you can never step into the same stream of consciousness twice. You don't have the exact same personality, or even the same "deeply held convictions," for long. Therefore, if consciousness were the self, you could never be exactly the same person from one moment to the next.

While it may seem counterintuitive to say that you aren't the same person now that you will be in the future, it's simply a consequence of the fact that you undergo constant changes throughout your life, and you do not have any kind of "self" that makes you the same person through time. You could be an infinity of "selves" throughout life, but not have any true, consistent self.

To be clear, saying that your *self* does not exist does not imply that *you* as a being do not exist. If everything about you can change without your losing your sense of selfhood, then the self cannot actually *be* anything. But whether *you* are real is an entirely separate question from whether you have a real self.

But if there is no core self, how can we still feel a self? It is possible to have a sense of self without having an actual self. The sense of self is really the feeling that something inherently *you* has persisted through time. This simply isn't true, but that doesn't prevent us from having a perception of being the same person and having connectedness through life. In fact, everything that we identify as making up our self could be taken away from us without us losing a sense of selfhood. Therefore, while the self does not exist, what does exist for us is the sense of having and being a self.

What makes us feel as if we have a self is that something gives us the impression of being the same person throughout time. One theory is that we derive this sense largely from the way the mind interprets memories. So then, we think that we existed at a past time not because we have all the same physical or mental features, but rather because we have the unique capability to remember *being* that person at one time. Similarly, what connects us to our future and gives us a sense that we will be the same person later is the knowledge the person in the future will be the sole bearer of our experiences, who will know what it was like to be us at the present time.

While talking about memory as the source of the sense of self is logical, if we tried to make memory the origin of self, rather than of the *sense* of self, we have several absurd resulting implications. For instance, if memory were the self, then if you could not remember a time during your life, your self did not exist at that time. Furthermore, memory is highly inaccurate. Therefore, even if your memory made you yourself, then the self would still be an illusion, because it would be based on inaccurate *perceptions* of the past.

But why do we feel something that does not exist? The sense of self is not just a feeling of persisting through time, but of having certain characteristics through time. However, these characteristics of self are a fabrication of your mind, produced by the brain's inherent tendency to search for patterns. Psychologist Susan Blackmore believes that though we are constantly changing, we conjure up a sense of self from an attempt to find connection between our experiences. Consequently, she says that we create the illusion of continuity "only when [we] look for it" (Kuhn).

Think of your individual memories as points on a scatter plot. Your brain's natural tendency to produce patterns creates a metaphorical "line of best fit" through these points. The line of best fit represents the correlation between our memories and our behavior, forming our beliefs about ourselves. According to neuroscientist Sam Harris, the sense of self is like a narrative that we form from the input of all our remembered experiences in order to explain our thoughts and behavior to ourselves (Hood).

Philosopher Daniel Dennet from Tufts University believes that "opposing processes in the brain, which tend to abhor inconsistency" create the narrative of self in order to explain the incongruities in our thoughts and behavior. As we engage in confirmation bias (the tendency to discard information that doesn't conform to our expectations) when regarding our past, the idea of a self becomes a necessary way of disregarding and unifying some pieces of information. In this idea of self, the sense of self has nothing to do with a real understanding of who we are. Rather, it's a mental device that masks our lack of experiential unity (Kuhn).

While these ideas of self may be supported by recent research, the theory that the sense of self emerges from perceived patterns is certainly not new. Even the 1800s transcendentalist philosopher Ralph Waldo Emerson spoke of something similar in describing the self, which he compares to a ship: "The voyage of the best ship is a zigzag line of a hundred tacks. See the line from a sufficient distance, and it straightens itself to the average tendency" (Emerson). Again, the idea is that the sense of self emerges from a need to find unity in our disunities.

Self cannot exist because we have no temporal uniformity. A sense of self must exist because we crave an illusion of consistency. But if the sense of self forms from patterns the brain sees in our behavior, doesn't that mean that we should have a fairly accurate sense of who we are? Not necessarily.

According to the *Scientific American,* "Most of us think that we are better than we actually are ... in every way" (Atasoy). Cornell University researchers have found that, "people typically believe they are more likely to engage in selfless, kind, and generous behaviors than their peers, a result that is both logically and statistically suspect." Further, "people on average tend to think they are more charitable, cooperative, considerate, fair, kind, loyal, and sincere than the typical person." This is not because we have a gratuitously dark view of our peers. In fact, if you're like most people, your opinions of others are more accurate than your view of yourself (Epley and Dunning 861).

Furthermore, studies have found that you also have an inflated opinion of your own competence: "93 percent of drivers rate themselves as better than the median driver. Of college professors, 94 percent say that they do above-average work … Stock pickers think the stocks they buy are more likely to end up winners than those of the average investor." Finally, if you think that you, at least, are more realistic about yourself than other people are, you're not alone. Most people tend to believe that they give more accurate self-assessments than others — a statistical impossibility (Atasoy).

If the sense of self is so horribly flawed, why does the brain bother to create it at all? As it turns out, our sense of self is actually quite useful, not in spite of — but rather, because of — its many inaccuracies. We only need to perceive ourselves at all because there are multiple evolutionary benefits to perceiving ourselves incorrectly. Since people are social beings, it's advantageous for us to convey to others that we have desirable characteristics, like above average levels of altruism. The most efficient way for a social organism to convey this information is to have an inflated ego.

Trying to deceive others about our positive attributes is cognitively taxing, since we have to maintain both a concept of who we are and whom we want other people to think we are. Furthermore, most people are fairly good at detecting attempts at deception, and tend to respond quite negatively to deceptive people. To convince others of our desirable traits while inflicting the minimum cognitive load on ourselves, the most effective method the brain can employ is merely altering the sense of self to incorporate those qualities we need others to think that we have.

Additionally, having a higher opinion of yourself increases your confidence. This is important because, as the *Scientific American* explains, confidence "plays a role in determining whom people choose as leaders and romantic partners. Confident people are believed more and their advice is more likely to be followed" (Atasoy). This means that we have another evolutionary incentive to create enhanced self-perceptions.

Therefore, even though logically, we can conclude the self does not exist, the sense of self will always be present. If you are aware only of your own perceptions — regardless of how accurate those perceptions are — then, in a way, your illusion of self is the most real "self" you have. However, the inconsistency of identity and the illusionary nature of the self make your self-concept malleable. Recognizing that self is an illusion allows you to take full advantage of the sense of self for what it really is — a social tool.

If your sense of self is really just formed by your memories of yourself, then you only think that you are a certain kind of person because you can remember behaving a particular way. But these perceptions are not fixed; they don't even have to be lodged in reality. Therefore, you could really create any sort of "self" you want.

If we reach our conclusions about our various selves by observing our past behavior, the corollary is that if we alter the way we behave, we can change our sense of self. As mentioned earlier, researchers could manipulate people's opinions simply by convincing them that they'd given a certain answer during a survey. Similarly, we can manipulate the sense of self by acting as if we possess characteristics we desire. According to *The Guardian*, "If you want to think of yourself as generous — or happy or confident or patient — then act how generous people act; the self-perception will follow" (Burkeman).

Intentionally taking advantage of the brain's tendency to exaggerate your assets can improve your performance on anything from standardized testing to a job interview (McCorquodale). According to *Mental Floss*, "Trying to fake your way to success seems dubious at best and delusional at worst. And yet, there is plenty of science that proves you can actually fool yourself and others into becoming more successful, finding love, and increasing your happiness." Something as simple as adopting a more confident posture increases your sense of power and causes others to view you as a more competent, assertive person. You can even generate emotions (such as happiness or romantic interest) simply by pretending to feel them (McCorquodale).

Can you know yourself? The self is an enigma, a perception, and a useful fallacy. You can't truly know yourself, and you may not even have a self to know. But not knowing yourself can actually be a good thing. To some extent, the art of self-deception even has the power to transform you into the kind of person you pretend to be. The self may be a figment of the imagination, but at least we have the power to choose our own illusion.

Works Cited

Atasoy, Ozgun. "You are Less Beautiful Than You Think You Are." *Scientific American*. Springer Nature. 21 May 2013.

Burkeman, Oliver. "This column will change your life: self-perception theory." *The Guardian*. Guardian News and Media Limited, 5 Oct. 2012.

Emerson, Ralph Waldo. "Self-Reliance." *Texts: Essays: First Series: SELF-RELIANCE*. Emerson Central. 1841.

Epley, Nicholas, and David Dunning. "Feeling 'Holier Than Thou': Are Self-Serving Assessments Produced by Errors in Self- or Social Prediction?" *Journal of Personality and Social Psychology*, vol. 79, no. 6, American Psychological Association, 2000, p. 861.

Goldhill, Olivia. "You're a completely different person at 14 and 77, the longest-running personality study ever has found." *Quartz*. Quartz, 1 Mar. 2017.

Hood, Bruce. "What is the Self Illusion?" *Psychology Today*. Sussex Publishers, LLC., 23 May 2012.

Kuhn, Robert Lawrence. "Is Your 'Self' Just an Illusion?" *Live Science*. Purch. 7 Sept. 2016.

McCorquodale, Amanda. "8 'Fake It 'Til You Make It' Strategies Backed by Science." *Mental Floss*. Mental Floss. 2 Feb. 2016.

The Sacred and Secular Soul

Andrea Savage

I remember the day he died. Struck by a drunk driver a week after his eighteenth birthday, the doctors pronounced him dead on the evening of July 4th, 2014. But it was not in that moment, when they unhooked the machines that unnaturally pumped oxygen into lungs and the IVs that bloated his lanky body that he died. He never made it to the hospital. Though his body remained, Tim was gone. And he had been, since the evening of July 3rd, 2014 on the fateful bicycle ride home. We sat in the hospital for fifteen hours hoping and praying it wasn't true, but, in our hearts, we knew better. For the body is not in charge of its own fate, but, rather, the soul. When the soul has lost its will to survive, when the soul is tired, and when the soul decides life is done, the body obeys—reluctantly, at first, but it always succumbs in the end.

This word "soul" is so casually used, implying many different things—a state of mind, a life force, a being, a feeling, and a friend. "Soul" is used in place of person, existence, and experience. The word is used for the inanimate, such as soul music and food. To be a soul is to be a human. You may wonder, "Does the soul even exist, or is it merely a synonym of humanity?" That all-important question, however, may be unanswerable. As an intangible, transcending belief, the soul is impossible to quantify or pinpoint, and the question is irrelevant because many people believe in the existence of some form of soul. It affects their identities, how they relate to one another, and how they find meaning and purpose in life regardless.

Throughout time and across schools of thought, the idea of the soul has helped people better understand themselves and grapple with their identity. For example, psychologist Carl Jung developed the theory of archetypes to help himself and his patients better understand the human soul. Some of these archetypes were things such as the anima and animus, the shadow, and the self. The anima was described as the "feminine" side to each male; the emotional, nurturing, and protective nature expressed through their personality. The animus was described as the opposite; the "masculine" logical and rational aspect of every woman. The Self, which Jung references as the "God within us" (Sharp), was described as the past, present, and future personality of a person. Finally, the Shadow was described as the hidden, unconscious aspects of identity, both good and bad, which the Self has—for any reason—decided not to express or does not recognize (Sharp). These major soul archetypes helped Jung address the mental anguishes of his patients and help them understand their own identity.

Additionally, many philosophers and poets have tried to explain how the soul relates to identity. Philosopher René Descartes believed "man was a union of the body and the soul, each a distinct substance acting on the other" (qtd. in Soul). More recently, philosopher Mark Goldblatt describes the placement and existence of the soul as an aspect of our identity. He describes the process of amnesia, beginning by being struck over the head and forgetting pertinent details about one's self. He describes the things the person may forget: likes and dislikes, close relatives, friends, and speech. Even more major things, depending on the severity of the injury, such as belief systems, values, gender, name, and personality may be impacted. These characteristics commonly thought of as identity are stripped from the person suffering amnesia, but Goldblatt postulates these things are not identity:

> It's tempting to conclude that, minus those characteristics, I would no longer be me. But in truth, that's all I would be. The human soul, if it exists in an immaterial form, must be the me-ness of me, the sense of first personhood on which the rest of my conscious experiences hang. It's the rooting interest each one of us has in himself, in his own existence, stripped of language and memory, stripped of thought and disposition; it's the unified presence by which I differentiate myself from whatever I encounter. I am not the thing I encounter; I am the thing doing the encountering. (Goldblatt)

Further, Goldblatt describes the soul—not as consciousness—but beyond it, an immaterial entity working in cohesion with a material brain. Goldblatt places the soul in the brain, giving it credit for aiding in memory creation and emotion. This means that, if the soul exists, it is the very basic foundation of our identity and cannot be stripped away entirely. It is what supersedes memory, emotion, and even death.

In addition to our identity, the concept of soul establishes how we relate to one another. In religions such as Christianity, Judaism, and Islam, the soul is uniform. For Christians, the soul is God-breathed, and, in effect, God in us (*English Standard Version*, Genesis 2:7). In his essay "The Over-Soul", Ralph Waldo Emerson, the American essayist and poet, says "There is no screen or ceiling between our heads and the infinite heavens, so is there no bar or wall in the soul where man, the effect, ceases, and God, the cause, begins" (Emerson). This would involve a commonality between all of mankind. Despite our differences in DNA, experience, and background, we all have a single, God-breathed soul which unites us all and gives us common ground with one another.

In Ancient Greece, a soul was believed to dwell in all living things: plants, beasts, and humans (*Ancient Theories of Soul*). The idea of a shared soul between all living things helps us perceive beauty in nature, as opposed to merely function. It may be the reason we connect with animals and nature; the reason why places and objects can hold so much meaning.

Buddhists theorize the interconnection between individuals, their environment, and others as all being deeply connected. The self creates the environment, and one cannot live without the other. Each person creates their environment to project their soul, allowing themselves the life they believe they deserve (The Oneness). Furthermore, notable theoretical physicist Albert Einstein, in a letter to a grieving father of similar faith, wrote on the unification of life:

> A human being is a part of the whole, called by us "Universe", a part limited in time and space. He experiences himself, his thoughts and feelings as something separated from the rest — a kind of optical delusion of his consciousness. The striving to free oneself from this delusion is the one issue of

true religion. Not to nourish the delusion but to try to overcome it is the way to reach the attainable measure of peace of mind. (Einstein)

In other words, Einstein believed we were each part of the Universe, and should see ourselves beyond the constraints of time and space. While he does not specifically mention the soul, he hints at the possibility of something that transcends the "delusion" of separateness and obtains peace of mind and community with one another.

Finally, the idea of the soul helps give purpose and meaning to those who believe in it. With the deeper understanding of identity and the sense of uniformity with the world comes a stronger sense of connection and accountability to the world around you. For some religions, this means proselytizing, and sharing their beliefs with others. Many religions also believe in the immortality of the soul, that even after the body dies the soul lives on, "And the dust returns to the earth as it was, and the spirit returns to God who gave it" (*English Standard Version,* Eccl. 12:7). The implication of this gives an intense meaning of how and for what they live, both in the mortal life and the immortal one.

For psychologists who believe in the soul, it helps provide a secular meaning to lives. For Jung, the understanding that the soul gives meaning to life provides hope to mentally distraught patients:

But what will he do when he sees only too clearly why his patient is ill; when he sees that it arises from his having no love, but only sexuality; no faith, because he is afraid to grope in the dark; no hope, because he is disillusioned by the world and by life; and no understanding, because he has failed to read the

meaning of his own existence? *(Modern Man in Search of a Soul*
260)

For every individual, whether they believe in the soul or not, it
implies a deeper level of accountability to fellow man and a connection
between all people. For even if we are all soul-less masses, a collection
of particles in a place with no purpose, we are all somehow connected.
We all exist, and therefore have existence. For many, the soul gives
meaning to that existence and a hope for the future.

In conclusion, "All goes to show that the soul in man is not an
organ, but animates and exercises all the organs.... [I]t is not the
intellect, or the will, but the master of the intellect and the will. It is the
vast background of our being . . . an immensity not possessed and that
cannot be possessed" (Emerson). Though incomprehensible and
unquantifiable, the soul defines identity, creates connection, and gives
purpose and meaning to many people. Whether you believe in it or not,
the idea of the soul contributes every day to our existence,
communicating with our brains and our hearts to give us our sense of
identity, our place, and our purpose.

Works Cited

Einstein, Albert. "On Being." *Letters of Note*, 12 Feb. 1950,

www.lettersofnote.com/2011/11/delusion.html. Accessed 3 May

2017.

Emerson, Ralph W. *The Over-Soul.* 4th ed., vol. 1, New York City, The

Norton Anthology, 1994, pp. 1062-73.

Jung, Carl G. *Modern Man in Search of a Soul.* London, Broadway House,

1933, pp. 248-60.

Ojibwa, "The Soul." *The Native American Netroots*, The Native American

Netroots, 19 Nov. 2011, nativeamericannetroots.net/diary/1148.

Accessed 20 Apr. 2017.

Sharp, Daryl. "Jung Lexicon." *The Jung Page*, Reflections on Psychology,

Culture, and Life, 27 Oct. 2013, www.cgjungpage.org/learn/jung-

lexicon. Accessed 1 Mar. 2017.

"Soul." *Encyclopædia Britannica*, Encyclopædia Britannica, inc., 25 Feb.

2010, https://www.britannica.com/topic/soul-religion-and-

philosophy. Accessed 19 Apr. 2017.

"Stanford Encyclopedia of Philosophy." *Ancient Theories of Soul*,

Standford University, 22 Apr. 2009,

https://plato.stanford.edu/entries/ancient-soul/#6. Accessed 20

Apr. 2017.

The Bible. English Standard Version, Crossway, 2017

"The Oneness of Life and its Environment." *Soka Gakkai International*,

Soka Gakkai International, Jan. 2017, www.sgi.org/about-

us/buddhism-in-daily-life/oneness-of-self-and-environment.html.

Accessed 3 May 2017.

Oh, What Am I Doing Here?
Kori Little

I know I am an hour early. I timed everything to the minute because I am afraid to be late on the first day. Then in a fit of panic I ask myself: "Oh, what am I doing here?" I planned which parking lot and the entrances I would use. I came to the school several times to know the location of my classrooms ("Oh, what am I doing here?"). I have my new backpack filled with pencils, color coordinated folders and notebooks. I have all my books and materials for each class ("Oh, what am I doing here?"). I am a secure, stable, self-confident grown-up, so why am I terrified? My belly is fluttering; my mouth is dry ("Oh, what am I doing here?"). Everyone around me is so young and they seem to know what to do. Nobody else acts nervous ("Oh, what am I doing here?"). It's time for class and the teacher wants us to log on to the computers. Everyone is logging on and I don't know how ("Oh, what am I doing here?"). A nice young girl offers to show me what to do. I type all my information into the online program the teacher had set up for homework and I feel confident. I click save: I spelled my name wrong. "Oh, what am I doing here?"

This was how the beginning of my terrifying first day at college started at the age of fifty. I was faced with apprehension, insecurities, misconceptions, and uncertainty about my abilities and knowledge. At some point, we all come across circumstances that test our self-concept or cause us to question our self-identity. These can be very difficult, as mine was, but our reaction to the circumstances is important to a healthier and continuously developing self. Ultimately, it is how we embrace challenges and various experiences that leads to a stronger self.

First, to figure out what influences and experiences impact the self, an understanding of self is beneficial. Self-concept is one portion of self that can be affected by experiences. Self-image, self-esteem, and ideal self are the three components of self-concept according to American psychologist Carl Rogers (Cherry). Self-image is how we perceive our personality, physical traits, and social role. Self-esteem is how confident we feel, how we value ourselves, and the degree we respect ourselves. Our ideal self is how we wish we were. How we see our self may not always be the same as how we would like our self to be (Cherry). This means our self-concept is a mixture of how we see ourselves, how much we value ourselves, and how we would like to be. Self-concept is our own perceptions of who we are and not how others see us. I see myself as a quirky, opinionated, bossy, and loving person. I would like to see myself without the bossy part of my personality.

Second, self-identity is another portion of self that can be affected by experiences. Understanding self-identity can help us recognize how it is affected. Self-identity is similar to self-concept considering it includes self-esteem, how we value ourselves, as a component. According to psychologist and life coach Dr. Andrew Dobson, it also consists of world view, self-identity boundary, and self-assessments of our past, present, and future selves (Dobson). World view is a "vague set of rules and guidelines that we have unconsciously adopted from the life experiences and influences" that allow us to judge ourselves and the world around us (Dobson). The self-identity boundary is the self-defined limits of what actions and behavior we find acceptable from others and ourselves. Self-assessments allow us to use the past as a guideline for the present and use the past and present to help us decide what we want our self to be in the future (Dobson). In other words, our self-identity is the way we assess and value ourselves surrounded by a set of acceptable behavior rules that regulate our moral filter throughout life. Life experience has taught me the importance of hard work, dedication, and kindness. I have set this world view and self-identity boundary for myself and have the same expectations of others. For me self-assessment was focused on my lack of college education and the future was easy: I wanted a college education.

The next step, with the explanations of self in mind, is to look at when the development of self begins. The development of self starts when we are children and continues to develop as we get older. Factors like our surroundings, our successes and our failures, and people we encounter during our childhood impact the development of our self-concept and self-identity in either a positive or negative way ("Self-Esteem"). Professor of pediatrics and psychiatry Michael Lewis believes that children start to realize they have a separate self and begin to grasp their relation to the world around age two months. This is the time children will begin to learn optimism and pessimism (McLeod). An example of children beginning to realize they have a self is when they react to a voice or mimic a gesture. When a child receives positive feedback for a smile it reinforces optimism and when there is no feedback or a negative response the child will learn pessimism. Children's understanding of their age, size, gender, or place in a family are starting points for development of self. For example, I talk, sing, and coo at my grandchildren from the minute they are born and tell them how loved they are. I pick them up, kiss them, and encourage them to try again when they fall. It is fun to see them learn that their mom is my daughter and figure out their relationship to other members of the family.

Additionally, as our self is developing, we are trying to comprehend and define who we are. In the article "The Multiple Parts of Self," Gerald Young Ph.D. tells us "young people are trying to establish their roles, responsibilities, and sense of self . . . and [the self] keeps growing in one way or another" and our self is actively looking for new ways to grow. As children, we begin to develop our world view, our life guidelines for judgments, from our experiences with family, friends, and social groups (Dobson). Self-concept is more flexible when we are younger and still learning who we are, and self-concept becomes more detailed as we age and figure out what is important to us (Cherry). Interactions between family and family traditions, political views, and religious ceremonies help with the development of self. If your parents exhibit certain family values those values will be incorporated into your base world view. If you are raised in a certain religion and belief system, you tend to build on that as a base. For example, I had a close relationship with my grandmother; she was a loving, strong, self-confident woman. She was a guiding factor in building my base world view when I was young. When my self was being established and looking for new ways to grow she demonstrated the value of family, how to be kind, and to work hard. These influences on my developing world view and self-concept started when I was young and continued into adulthood.

As the self continues to develop it can be shaped, altered, and repaired by positive environmental factors throughout life. American psychologist Carl Rogers believed children that were shown unconditional love by their parents developed a healthier self-concept than children who had to earn love and acceptance (Cherry). Rogers also believed that a person "who receive[s] nonjudgmental support and love can develop the self-esteem and confidence to be the best person they can be and live up to their full potential." This usually happens during childhood but can happen at any point in life (Cherry). Positive experiences like "being listened to, being spoken to respectfully, having accomplishments be recognized and mistakes or failures be acknowledged and accepted," lead to increasing our self-concept and self-identity ("Self-Esteem"). Someone who is given unconditional love and support, like my grandmother gave me, would most likely have a more positive self. She always told me how much I was loved and encouraged me even when I didn't do the right thing or I failed at something. A general feeling of worthiness and a strong world view would be the lasting effects of this unconditional love and provide the base for a stable and strong self.

Beyond unconditional love, there are other ways to actively strengthen our self against negative factors and promote a positive self. As humans, we "possess an inherent need to grow and achieve [our] potential" of a stable and healthy self (Cherry). Understanding your self-identity and how you fit in the world "allows you to examine who you are and more importantly create who you want to be" (Dobson). Finally, the ability to accurately assess and accept our self, for all its weaknesses and strengths, leads to a healthier self ("Self-Esteem"). Starting college at the age of fifty was my self wanting to grow and achieve my potential. I did not want to be stagnant in who I am and my role in the world. I was certain I had the potential to be something better than my current self.

Although we are continually trying to build a strong self, or even when we feel it is completely established, there will come a time when challenges cause us to actively assess our self. This may be a major life event, a normal progression of age, or the quest to find out who we are. It could be a decision we made or a situation out of our control. Negative or stressful challenges can cause anxiety, insecurities, apprehension, uncertainty, or even misconception about ourselves and others. According to Dobson, *"life, people, events and circumstances are consistently random and unpredictable – and certainly not designed for your best interests all the time." Criticism, abuse, ridicule, expectations of perfection, and viewing failures as a defining characteristic can have a negative impact on the self* ("Self-Esteem"). *I consider myself to have an established self. However, when faced with the apprehensions about attending college, fear of failure and the unknown, my self-concept and self-identity were challenged. It caused me nervousness and doubt about my ability to learn and do the school work.*

Luckily, all difficult experiences are not guaranteed to have a negative impact on self-concept and self-identity. A stable and secure self can minimize the difficult circumstances and the severity of their impact on the self. According to the article "Who am I? Self Identity –

How to Build Personal Character," when a person is faced with events that could have a negative impact on self they will make "decisions based on [their] boundaries, and it increases [their] sense of self-esteem and makes a stronger ... self-identity" (Dobson). Since I had a strong self before beginning school, I could make the decision to stay true to my base self and still further develop my self-identity. I needed to remember who I was as a person and not let the challenge of college harm my self-concept and self-identity long term.

In fact, it is our decision to determine whether the impact of the challenges is temporary or long lasting. The bearing a circumstance has on our self may last a few moments, long term, or even cause a permanent change in our self. An influence that causes a "drop in confidence will lower self-esteem in the short term. Prolonged negative experience will produce a longer term reduction of self-esteem" and the same is true for positive experiences (Dobson). For people with healthy self-esteem, the everyday events that bring on anxiety will only cause a temporary impact. However, those with a lower self-esteem will see a greater and more lasting impact ("Self-Esteem"). By building a solid, healthy self the impact of negative experience can be shortened. My self-esteem was lowered due to uncertainty and fear of failure in the beginning, but I started with a strong and healthy self-esteem, so I reverted to my healthy self-esteem in a short amount of time. Since the drop in confidence was only temporary I was able to focus on school and not the effects of a lowered self-esteem. For me, the future was easy: I wanted a college education.

Ultimately our reaction to the challenge and its possible impact can determine the longevity and severity of the impact on our self. When the self is faced with possible negative circumstances the "resulting emotional experience you have from [the] situation, person or event is then determined by how well you managed the experience in relation to your world view" and self-concept (Dobson). Being open to experiences, not becoming defensive, being able to assess challenges and experiences correctly, and being open to feedback with the willingness to make real changes are characteristics that create positive reactions to circumstances that may otherwise have a negative impact on the self (Cherry). On the first day of school I could have given up when I spelled my name wrong. I was discouraged and could have just determined school was not for me. Instead I took on the challenge, studied hard, and was determined to do my best. There will more challenges as I continue in college, however I will access those situations as they come and use my healthy world view and self-identity boundary of hard work, dedication, and kindness to lessen the impact of the challenges.

Determining our reaction to experiences may be the hardest part of developing a healthy self. Once something happens to undermine our self we must find ways to alter our reaction to reduce the negative impact on our self or causing them to have a positive impact. There are steps that can be taken to repair any negative and lasting effects of low self-esteem. Begin by challenging "negative messages of the critical inner voice" and recognizing we are all humans that make mistakes and are not perfect ("Self-Esteem"). Also, even though asking for help may be difficult, locate and utilize a support system of friends, groups, teacher, coworkers, counselors, pastors, and family ("Self-Esteem"). In the GoodTherapy.org article "Self-Esteem," the authors state that "finding a sense of accomplishment is a huge boost to self-esteem . . . and identify[ing] specific activities that boost confidence and competence" will help repair and build a healthier self (Warkentin-Houdek et al). The article further explains that experiences of unconditional love, encouragement, and respect will help speed up the process of healing the self (Warkentin-Houdek et al). Even with many instances of negative experiences there is hope for repair. Given that I had not been to school in over thirty years, it was important that I realize that it is fine not to be perfect and ask for help when I need it. Relying on the support and encouragement of family and friends gives me confidence to do my best and allow for possible unsuccessful moments. I also sought out the advice of professors and consider them to be valuable mentors.

Furthermore, it is important to remember that embracing new challenges will provide the opportunity to grow and strengthen our self. According to professor of psychology Gerald Young the self wants to grow and "reach[es] out in new directions without you being aware of it...or you might take a very open decision to seek out new directions in self-growth and explore new avenues in the self" (Young). Young explains that our self is constantly looking new for areas to grow and develop even when the self appears to be stable and secure. Embracing the challenge of school allows me to enjoy college. I still have my color coordinated folders and binders because these simple things give me comfort. However, I am willing to take risks with harder classes when initially I would have been too insecure and apprehensive.

By embracing the challenges to our self, we enrich all aspects of our life. The benefits of a healthier world view and self-identity boundary provide a stronger version of our self. Someone with a healthy self is "able to live fully in the moment . . . because they experience a sense of inner freedom and embrace creativity, excitement and challenges" (Cherry). Someone who embraces challenges to the self can interact well with others, has a flexible self-concept, and has the ability to trust their own values and form new or amended values according to new experiences (Cherry). When a person can live in the moment, they are allowing themselves "free[dom] to be spontaneous without fearing" rejection and embrace the challenges knowing there is growth (Cherry). Even though embracing challenges to the self is scary, understanding the potential for growth outweighs the fear. Getting a new job, starting college, starting a family, moving to a different city, or joining a club can be rewarding challenges that strengthen our self-concept and self-identity.

As our self is developing we all come across circumstances that test our self-concept or cause us to question our self-identity. Our self begins to develop at an early age and continues as we get older. Developing a strong self allows for healthier reactions to negative experiences. The reaction to outside influences is possibly the most important determination of a healthier and continuously developing self. The more we embrace challenges and various experiences the stronger our self can become. My first day of college was a challenge. Because I saw myself as a secure person, I was confused and thrown off balance by my insecurities and apprehensions. Now when I ask: "Oh, what am I doing here?" I can answer: Learning to embrace the new challenge of college. "Oh, what am I doing here?" I am becoming a good student and figuring out my abilities. "Oh, what am I doing here?" I am learning, growing, having fun at school. I am teaching my children and grandchildren they can do anything. "Oh, what am I doing here?" I am meeting, appreciating, and admiring new people. I am making friends in many age groups. "Oh, what am I doing here?" I am building a stronger self. I am building a self to be proud of.

Works Cited

Cherry, Kendra. "What Is Self-Concept and How Does It Form?" *verywell.com*. 31 Aug. 2016. www.verywell.com/what-is-self-concept-2795865. Accessed 13 Mar. 2017.

Dobson, Andrew. "Who am I? Self-Identity-How to Build Personal Character." *Mindfit Hypnosis*. 2013. www.mindfithypnosis.com/who-am-i-self-identity.

McLeod, Saul. "Self Concept." *SimplyPsychology.org*. Simply Psychology. 2008. www.simplypsychology.org/self-concept.html.

"Self-Esteem." *University of Texas Counseling and Mental Health Center*. 2017. cmhc.utexas.edu/selfesteem.html. Accessed 10 Mar. 2017.

Warkentin-Houdek, Nancy, et al. "Self-Esteem." *GoodTherapy.org*. 23 Sep. 2016. Accessed 10 Mar. 2017.

Young, Gerald. "The Multiple Parts of the Self: Leading Yourself to the Stage of Growth." Psychology Today. 17 Mar. 2011. www.psychologytoday.com/blog/rejoining-joy/201103/the-multiple-parts-the-self. Accessed 10 Mar. 2017.

Contributing Authors

Trystan Burris is pursuing a degree in education at Ozarks Technical community college. He will transfer to Missouri State University, where he already participates in the band program, and will major in music education.

Kendra Caruso is a mother to two lovely children, Kira and Kitt, and just celebrated twelve years of marriage to her husband Billy. She is earning her Associate's degree in Biology, serves as the Secretary on the Honors Student Council at OTC, and works part-time with Mad Science teaching kids. Kendra is lucky to have received her nature and her nurture from her wonderful and supportive parents, Kent and Peggy, who have always encouraged her to chase her dreams in life.

Cally Chisholm is currently pursuing an Associate of Arts degree at OTC, and plans to transfer to another college for Journalism and Graphic Design. When she's not blending concretes at Andy's Frozen Custard or being the media intern at her church, she enjoys binge watching Netflix and volunteering.

J. Abigail Cool is an Honors Student at OTC and has been accepted into the Behavioral Health Support program with the Allied Health Department with hope of graduation in the summer of 2018 where she will begin working with and helping people discover preventative measures to end generational and cyclical patterns of violence. Abigail loves gardening, raising sheep, tending a farm, and being the mother of five grown children (and her beloved Sheltie, Sophie).

Viktoriia Hryshchenko is an international student from Ukraine. She is pursuing her dream in getting a Behavioral Sciences degree. If the dream is not accomplished, she's always wanted to be an eggplant farmer.

Jana Kim is a 20-year-old Korean-American college student majoring in entertainment management. She was born and raised in Springfield, MO and attended Kickapoo High School. She hopes that with her major, she can bring more diversity into the entertainment field.

Dayton Kingore is a college student in Springfield, Missouri. He is the oldest of five children. Dayton hopes to graduate with a degree in accounting.

Kori Little is an ASCP certified Histotechnician and Specialist in Laboratory Safety for a hospital anatomic pathology laboratory. She plans to get her Associate of Science in Biology degree at OTC and then attend Drury University for her Bachelor of Science degree. Kori enjoys crafts, playing with her grandchildren, and digging her toes in the sand on beach vacations.

Brady Marshall is an autistic student of Ozarks Technical Community College in Springfield, Missouri, where he plans to get an Associate of Arts Transfer degree to Missouri State University. He was born and raised in Southwest Missouri and diagnosed with autism at two years of age. Some of his hobbies are meditating, editing videos with Adobe software, walking around a park or recreation center, and contributing photos and comments to Google Maps.

Olivia Meyers is 21 years old, on her way to becoming a veterinarian and still trying discover her full identity.

Sarah Powell is pursuing her Associate of Arts at OTC. Majoring in art and minoring in illustration, she plans to become a professional illustrator and composer.

Hannah Quick is a soon-to-be college freshman. She has enjoyed taking dual-enrollment classes at OTC and looks forward to continuing her education at Vanderbilt University in fall 2017.

Ty E. Ragsdale was born in Joplin and raised in a rural area just outside of Springfield. He spends his days listening to, producing, and learning about music. He is also a coach at a local gymnastics gym.

Kathleen Ruffell is a student at Ozarks Technical Community College working toward her Bachelor's degree in Business Administration. She loves the outdoors along with activities like jet skiing, hiking and camping.

Andrea Savage is a 20-year-old born and raised in Springfield, MO. She is attempting to major in marketing, but that is subject to change. Her interests include the outdoors, music, and her family, preferably in combination.

David Vergel de Dios lives in Springfield, Missouri. He is pursuing a general degree with an emphasis in history. His current goal is to become a police officer in Springfield.

Lane Williamson is a 20-year-old-man who is attending college to get his Computer Information Systems Degree. He works in sales and spends his free time playing Rocket League (a video game where you play soccer with cars) competitively.

Hannah Winder is a current OTC Honor student who will be studying history at Missouri State University in the fall of 2017. She currently works at the public library in Bolivar, Missouri and spends most of her days between stacks of books.